TAILORED THINKERS
The Masters of Perception and Persuasion

By Colm Woods

Edited by Jessica Tabaqchali

ISBN: 9781080759026
Publishing: Kindle Direct Publishing by Amazon Books
Cover Art: Colm Woods

For publishing, sales, or copyright information, please contact:

information@tailoredthinkers.com

To contact the author for media, or other inquiries, please contact:

author@tailoredthinkers.com

To the writers, thinkers and doers who have inspired me, the curiosity that compels me, and the (~~clinical perfectionism~~) will that sustains me – thank you.

CONTENTS

TO READ A BOOK

"One of the symptoms of an approaching nervous breakdown is the belief that one's work is terribly important."

- Bertrand Russell

I didn't set out to write a book.

In fact, it wasn't too long ago that I just wanted to read one. A single book. Maybe this sounds familiar.

For my part, I was convinced that it was just a sign of modern times. Work was all-encompassing, the media cycle was endless, Netflix was too tempting, human interaction grew more and more digitized, and my concentration had fallen from tunnel-like focus to a distractible flicker. I was addicted to the immediacy of Google, gorged on the digestibility of tweets, and revelled in the disposability of blogs and videos. In that sphere, affirmation is immediate and the content, importantly, is free.

My bookshelf was empty, and my brain was full – or so it felt. But what was I denying myself as a result of this irrational fear of content commitment?

I had always been fascinated with language and words. School was mostly a joy, both my parents are teachers by profession, and I had grown up reading everything and anything I could to occupy myself on sleepless nights, rainy afternoons and long drives to visit grandparents.

If you had mentioned the word "iPad" back then, we would have blushed at the thought of a female sanitary device, so it was all football on the streets and books under bedside lamps in the late 1990s. Whether *Harry Potter*, *The Saga of Darren Shan* and

Lemony Snicket's *A Series of Unfortunate Events*, to my later adventures into the enthralling worlds of Orson Scott Card's *Ender's Game*, Harper Lee's *To Kill a Mockingbird* and J.G Ballard's *Empire of the Sun*, there was a time when I devoured entire series over a few weeks of summer holidays – a now distant life without the 'ping' (or pang) of smartphone dependency. And all of that was 'conventional' reading, just books.

By divorcing ourselves from the highfalutin idea that "reading" is some intellectually superior act of consuming critically-acclaimed books, we can appreciate there was far more "read" than I previously gave myself credit for.

I read the product details on shoeboxes, the washing instructions on clothing tags, the nutritional information on Kellogg's cereal multipacks, the headlines and photo captions on newspapers, the brand names and copywriting on every billboard, the 'open / closed' sign on every shop front, the badge on almost every passing car, the details on every sports crest...

the list goes on and on. Endlessly – it has never stopped – and I

know I'm not alone when I say that my appetite remains

increasingly, inconveniently insatiable.

Thinking about this more broadly, the effect on modern

communications practice has been profound. The ability to read,

and our incurable and ever-evolving human curiosity, has made

this world consumable. The last decade has seen a

transformative rise in both tension and overlap between

traditional reading and modern content consumption, and the

losers in this zero-sum game are consumers and creators alike.

As it turns out, we are not 'hard-wired' or 'conditioned' to accept

only this or that, short-form or long-form content. And despite

how difficult the first step back into books can be, the rewards

are honestly endless.

It was late August 2016, I had handed in my notice from agency-

life in Dublin, and I sought refuge in my first real book in over a decade. I never expected a GoodReads 4.3/5, 250-page book by acclaimed advertising executive and agency head David Trott to change my life.

I picked up *One+One = Three* because it was short, had oversized, double-spacing and it looked easy to finish. That was it. At the time, I was burnt out, fed up and increasingly disenfranchised with my career choice, naïvely hoping that reading a book about creativity would lift me out from a rut. Of course, it didn't immediately turn me into a creative genius, but a spark was lit. Once overwhelmed at the prospect of a 'full' book, I now curiously follow paths to psychology, anthropology, genetics, economics, politics, biography, business, creative writing, English grammar, more.

Trott was a vital dip of the proverbial toe, and suitably reignited a reading obsession that now includes audiobooks, YouTube discussions and obligatory airport bookstore purchases. The rest, as they say, is history.

I've now read about the complexity of Ant Colony Optimisation; and the rise of a new world order of AI superpowers. I'm engrossed by the pervasive rise of extremism and division within identity politics; could spot the difference between nouveau riche and the avant-garde. I know my gastrocnemius from my iliopsoas; the off-piste from the "OFF-WHITE"; can describe the differing construction of a made-to-measure suit from bespoke; and understand the role of jewels in the engineering of mechanical watches. At one point, I could easily name the sponsor and kit brand of every Premier League football team, and the exact boots of any player. At another, the top three car makes, models, and colours in every county in Ireland. Currently, my daily reading ranges from the websites Complex, Hodinkee and Balls.ie, to The Financial Times, The Economist and The Washington Post – critically including classical art puns and an extra helping of dog memes in between. And, as much for my own amusement as anyone else's, I am as likely to quote Derek Zoolander or Rick Sanchez as I am Descartes or Seneca. Somehow, I'm still shit at a Pub Quiz.

You see, I realized that I am *a consumer* – whatever form it takes. Think FOMO (Fear of Missing Out) – but on the comparative scale of standing outside on a wet afternoon in Dublin trying to catch every raindrop before it touches the ground. Impossible is nothing, according to Adidas. If only.

Clinically speaking, my personal penchant for information consumption is exacerbated by a more unfortunate predisposition, described by Sheva Rajaee, a psychotherapist at the OCD Center of Los Angeles, as obsessive thinking. My own psychiatrist, (an actual, qualified MD), diagnosed it as Generalized Anxiety Disorder – but I prefer Rajaee's YouTube friendly descriptor myself. In an easy to follow, annoyingly over-rehearsed, TedTalk in UCLA in June 2017, she perfectly, near-soothingly, concludes that "just because we don't know something, doesn't meant that we should go looking for it". I repeat: if only.

Today, on the other side of my literary renaissance, my concentration can still blow with the wind. My love of paperback books still ebbs and flows with the ups and downs of everyday life, I don't read a book a week, and I don't reach a target for a year. I am, for better or worse, a product of my digitally-dependent environment. Something I believe we all are, and the fact remains that it often takes a bit more will than it should to put down the screens and pick up a book.

Maybe you're finding the same trepidation in yourself now. Maybe you've already flicked ahead to check how many pages are to go. Maybe, just maybe, I can assure you that this book will be different. Why? Because I am you, and I was determined to write a book that someone like us would read.

Firstly, it's analogical. That means identifying and exploring outside ideas, systems, thinkers and examples to bring new meaning and understanding to our own little world of communications. And what that also means is that this will likely be the first book on the communications industry that doesn't use industry case studies – no Enron, no Malaysian Airlines, no BP oil spill, no Dove *Real Beauty*, and (the only one I'll actually miss) no Boaty McBoatface.

The world around us is changing at a pace few can match, and the industry has responded by segmentation and specialization – an outcome that I don't necessarily believe is positive. Silos fight for individual recognition, tools have been created to build a user-base rather than to solve problems, and we've descended from closely-knit industry to angry, budget-boasting armchair warriors. Undoubtedly, the complexity, scale and diversity of our professional challenges are rising, but what if the solutions were simple?

Changing times call for a change in approach, especially for anyone who makes a living in the various communications industries. The same tired examples of yesterday, while offering fair warning, fall far short of a toolkit for the challenges of today, never mind tomorrow. What we need is to look outside the box.

So, what has all this got to do with me?

Well, as unavoidable as it has been, everything. My anxiety is very specifically characterized by social anxiety, obsessive thinking and clinical perfectionism – depending on who you ask. The implications of this triple-threat multi-tool of cognitive characteristics actually provide a heightened understanding other people, interaction and implication, shaping my life and my career in communications to date.

With that at the forefront of my perspective, what follows in these chapters starts and ends with people.

Some of them you may already know – like Roman Emperor, Marcus Aurelius, the so-called godfather of modern PR, Edward Bernays, and Irish Taoiseach, Leo Varadkar – and other you may not have come across yet – ancient Greek mathematician, Eratosthenes, the founder of Judo, Jigoro Kano, and my Nana, Eileen Woods.

Either way, this is guaranteed to be a bullshit-busting, fact and fable-finding journey through an altogether-unconventional cartography of communications and public relations consultancy. And if that's too much of a mouthful, consider it an unfiltered look at the evolutionary and revolutionary communications challenges, opportunities, battles, and bridges we face – each with solutions far simpler than it may seem.

So, if that doesn't sound like your cup of tea, you can start scrolling through Instagram now...

CHAPTER ONE

OBSESSIVE CONSUMPTION

"The single biggest problem in communication is the illusion that

it has taken place."

- George Bernard Shaw

The world as we know it is more connected than ever. Content is the new currency, engagement offers endless potential for ecstasy, information is being communicated at fibre-optic speed, and we are absolutely fucking obsessed by the potential for more. The outcome? An addiction of epidemic proportions.

Exactly how much information is actively engaged with, processed (by people) and utilized in our everyday lives, remains to be seen. Do we create more than we need, accumulate more than we can ever comprehend, and rely too heavily on those who don't really understand? While the answers may seem abundantly clear, the questions raised by spiralling consumers and unchecked creators form the basis for where we must begin.

From the rise of the first digital futurists of the 1960s, through the digital adopters of the 1980s and 1990s, to digital natives of 2000s and 2010s, psychologists and researchers have comparatively mapped the rise of an obsession epidemic which has swept the now omnipotent digital age. The standard gateway concoction of Google, Instagram, Facebook, Snapchat and YouTube coalesce into pervasive streams that prod, probe and overwhelm the chemistry of our brains. Instant, endless, accessible.

As such, a distortion has occurred in the development of our psyches and our societies. The accumulative effect this continues to have on human consumption is likely out-dating every book on the subject to date. The counter-effect that it has on brand, corporate and political communication, to name just a few, is equally revolutionary and equally rapid.

What is clear, and will remain so, is that we as consumers and communicators are failing miserably to absorb and, importantly, manage this growth. You know it, and I know it, but the scale has reached levels that few among us can possibly grasp.

More information is written, captured and shared in a single social media minute than ever existed in thousands of years of human history. According to a 2018 Forbes report on the Internet of Things (IoT), there are 2.5 quintillion bytes of data created each day, and over 90 percent of the data in the world was generated in the last two years alone. To save you 'the Google', there are eighteen zeroes in quintillion... so that's 2,500,000,000,000,000,000 of those tiny units of digital information a day.

The unabashed reality of anything we invent to assist our communications is that we are indeed only human, no matter how many technological walls, lines and radio waves between us. The difference now is that, instead of being liberated by advances in technology, we are increasingly trapped in and defined by a life where incomprehensible levels of information create a world with less clarity than ever. To paraphrase a long-standing Irish anti-drink driving slogan, we simply don't "know the one that's one too many". We are addicts – the creators and consumers alike.

Everyone, from the nobody-actually-knows-what-age-bracket-it-refers-to Millennials, to the Facebook-is-for-creepy-old-people Generation Z, and all those haplessly categorized otherwise, is trying to find their way in a world where university education is deemed meaningless, anxiety has risen, and trust is eroded to almost non-existence – be that in the media, in politics, or in the person you went on three dates with and suddenly stopped replying to your DMs. Seemingly empirical scientific truths are more likely to be publicly dismissed by an ideological extremist on the news than explained by a "boring" academic or scientist; and computers, perhaps the only things capable of sorting all the information now available at the touch of a button, have nefariously progressed from the tool, to the crutch, to the leather-cushioned electric wheelchair of our ability to navigate daily life.

God forbid you have chosen a career in communications.

To complicate matters further still, within the industry, best practice has been hijacked and muddied by headline and profit-grabbing game-changers, self-proclaimed gurus and influencers, and increasingly-specialist specialists. The old heads are still editor-obsessed, but the mid-ranks would sell their first-born for 'reach' and industry newcomers think exclusively in followers. In many ways, the industry has become more unnecessarily complicated, self-serving and less impactful than ever. More concerned with awards, data, and applause, we've slipped from the right hand of CEOs and political leaders to the scoffed and scorned fluff-and-tumble of 'the PR people' – as if that's a shorthand for a jazz-hand twinkling dance troupe responsible for high-octane bouts of dazzle and distraction. Outside the confines of offices and organizations, the armchair experts are even worse.

Marketing gurus like Daniel Pink and Martin Lindstrom define the world in buying and selling – 'everyone is a consumer', 'to sell is human'. Gary 'Vee' Vaynerchuk says, "Fuck school!", drop out and be an entrepreneur. Most of the people you follow on Instagram want to show you "how to build a following" by getting perma-glistening six-pack abs, or by applying make-up, while they flog you an overpriced seven-day tea detox and a 'new clothing line' from the same Asian assembly line as half of their influencer friends.

Our world, our eyeballs, and now our profession has become clickbait.

Any advice you do seek out has become a sound bite, you've never met your mentors, and the successful people you wish to emulate "wake up like a Navy Seal", gorge on a diet of "hustle", and shit "paid partnerships". But how much of this career prescription is helpful? How much applicable? If you're a communications student, graduate, consultant, manager, or even an industry leader, I'd be willing to bet very little. Because Lindstrom, Pink and Vaynerchuk are over-amplified exceptions by design, who have invariably created the world they espouse. You are the consumer, you buy what they're selling, and they buy and sell access to your eyeballs.

Maybe, the advice that we (the communications profession) have been sold is not the advice we've needed. And yet, the advice we have to sell is more necessary than ever.

Traditional media readership and viewership has been plummeting for over a decade now. The keyboard warriors have changed the status quo. The trusted have become the untrustworthy and mass hysteria has infected every scroll of any screen we come across. What is said or done, is scrutinized and eternalized in the pixels and databases of our digitally dependent lives, and our times are defined by intense division, polarizing perceptions and zero-sum stances. It's easy to feel like communication has become an all or nothing affair.

Where did it all slip from our control? What can we do pull it back from the brink? What could we learn from stepping outside of the echo-chamber?

This book may not be the remedy, but it is the prognosis – a concerted effort to have a conversation at a time of unrelenting prescription. My hope is that it offers respite, clarity and solutions that manage to bridge and navigate the YouTubers, the authors, the academics, the media personalities, the consultants and the experiences of past and present that all shape our view of the world. This book draws on the experts, illuminators and straight talkers that have been responsible for shaping my personal take on our industry – views that remain entirely open for interpretation and challenge.

My goal for you, should you find value in these pages, is simply application and replication – not imitation. And I even promise (a little) less rhyming from here.

This book is not five-steps to the latest and greatest, neither is it a disposable product. It is a tool; a glimpse at the various professions of communication that have survived evolution and revolution of every individual communications hack to date. It will define the outer sphere of your role, help you to find your place in it, and give you the perspective to deliver at every level, in any situation you face.

How I got to the point of writing this book is anyone's guess. I don't have a blog, or a podcast, or 'a following'. But I have spent the last eight years studying and working in communications, having first stepped inside a PR agency at the fresh-faced age of eighteen. My initial goal was very simple: to find out what the fuck it actually was. Since then, there's been no coming back from it. I got my Bachelor's in Communications Studies, immediately added a Master's in Public Relations, and continued to learn and challenge myself with PR agency internships and SME side projects. To my obsessive, workaholic, perfection-seeking satisfaction, I soldiered the late nights, early mornings and endless demands, and loved every minute of it. I still do – in theory.

I've read almost every story there is to find about PR godfather, Edward Bernays, went full *Rain Man* on Grunig and Hunt's 'four models of public relations theory', designed national and international communications frameworks and strategies, and managed campaigns for internal, domestic, regional, international, crisis, brand, sport, sponsorship and political communications, all the while working with hundreds of communications professionals across three regions of the world to date.

In a given week since moving to work as a more specialist, strategic communications consultant in the Middle East, I have spoken to journalists for Tokyo TV in Japan, Al Arabiya in Riyadh, Reuters in Beirut, Bloomberg and CNN in Dubai, Sputnik in Moscow, The Australian in New South Wales, or France 24 in Paris. That in itself is just a small part of a role that includes working with senior politicians, management consultants and highly experienced colleagues to have developed and deliver national, regional and international communications programs around the world.

I will refer to my own experiences, where it helps to do so, but there are references from the wider world I've found to be far more interesting and illuminating than my own. Consider me, in many ways, a curator, and a messenger, with an overwhelming assertion that the communications profession – essential, tangible and valuable in its own right – is almost underwhelmingly simple in its function. No matter what you've been told and how mind-numbingly complex and convoluted it may seem.

TAILORED THINKERS is a distillation of what I've seen, what I've learned, and what you might learn from it. Starting as I intend to continue, let's take a communicator's look at the book have before you.

The title of the book is as simple and catchy as I could possibly manage. That's important for our low levels of attention and retention – remember? The name too should sound familiar. It's a deliberate play on the well-known, movie-adapted 1974 spy thriller, 'Tinker, Tailor, Soldier, Spy'. From there, a more pointed relevance begins to take shape.

Both words have double meaning. Consider it the positive equivalent of the proverbial ten pounds of shit in the five-pound bag, whatever that is.

"Tailored" refers to the bespoke approach to communications required to meet each individual challenge, but also serves as a not-so-subtle nod to my personal affliction for made-to-measure suits. "Thinkers", on the other hand, is a noun consciously or unconsciously typified by every person in the communications ecosystem. In order to make people do or feel or understand anything, you have to get them to think about it. In order to do that, you have to understand what they currently think, and why; what you'd like them to think, and how; and what success looks like; for who.

The contents of the book, then, are divided into two overarching themes, each building from the foundation established before it. Consider it a Mary Berry worthy sponge cake of personal and professional insight, without the need for perma-tanned Paul Hollywood's piercing blue eyes in accompaniment. Opening chapters seek to offer context to the changing landscape of our industry and our lives, in the hope of grounding our identity amid increasing existentialism. This groundwork allows us to drill deep into the core of who we are and where our value lies – professionally speaking, that is. I recommend you see someone far more clinically qualified for a wider assessment.

The remaining chapters target the more practical parts of our profession – the 'what', and even a little bit of the 'why', that spans far more of our work that we would dare to admit. We unpack why it's time to let go of the smoke and mirrors, the spin doctor caricatures, and the bullshit job titles, while we're at it. By starting the conversation, we have the opportunity to identify, understand and assess the many ways we might do better. Maybe even for the first time in a long time.

The approaches described are tried and tested for CEOs and multinationals, kings and nations, sports teams and local charity fundraisers. But before we get to those, we'll explore and unpack exactly what it means to be a consultant. The role to play. The life to lead. The success that can come. The pitfalls to avoid.

The relative success and joy that I've taken from this work has come from a bull-headed commitment to being channel agnostic, discipline diverse, and an all-rounder by design. A puritan, if you will. And through that, I've come to believe that whether you are a junior consultant or chief communications officer, a remote-flexi worker or officer lifer, an activist or just-getting-the-knack-of-this, there are universal themes and approaches for all manner of communications roles and professions. No matter where you are in the world, who you work for, and what message you're trying to push, it's all about taking, having or avoiding a role in basic human interactions at various levels of scale. That has never changed. So, ignore the latest guru, mogul or upstart trying to convince you otherwise. They are the true cloak and dagger merchants, who muddy waters with mystique, and conflate their success with a new world order. One "you too can learn", at a price... they claim.

As you can tell, I'm not buying that shit. I'm not even selling it. I'm just here to discuss how communications success is a goal-oriented and outcome driven thing that raises awareness, builds understanding, and/or elicits a response.

To suggest anything else is to put lipstick on a pig... when your goal is a bacon sandwich.

CHAPTER TWO

MILD-MANNERED MERCENARIES

"There are as many people as opinions"

- Irish proverb

I don't know how to describe what I do.

Yet somehow, it's all about helping others do just that – to find their voice, understand their audience, and tell their story, succinctly, honestly, clearly and consistently. You know, get to the crux of what they are really about in the hope of articulating it to others.

Maybe my inability to do this for my own role is why a single, innocent question from barista, taxi driver or even a loved one can evoke an imposter syndrome that claws at the skin in a way that would put Tom Hardy's *Venom* to shame. It's even worse when you're sheepishly guided to the next question, "Well, what does a normal day look like?". Fuck me, that's even worse. Has Brexit happened? Has someone pulled out of OPEC? Has there been progress on peace talks in Yemen? Have any negative stories tried to pull in our corporate client? Did they not ask for official comment? Was the presentation document finished? Was it printed? Is it Monday, or Saturday? Have I had a coffee yet?

What we do has been dressed in various titles, taking tens of functions and forms. But all the while, our purpose is singular – to be a trusted resource. An expert advisor in how our clients communicate with any one of the people or groups they care about.

Our role as advisors has always been about people. Individuals, groups; internal, external; domestic, international; public, or private; the greatest consultants orchestrate, influence and coordinate projects that have changed our lives more than we may ever realize. But all consultants, no matter how experienced, specialist, technical, talented, intelligent or creative, had to start by understanding a single person – themselves. Having outlined our ever-evolving sphere of operations in Chapter One, this second chapter shines the spotlight on who exactly we are, and just what the hell are we supposed to be doing.

A consultant is anyone hired to provide expert advice in a particular area. Usually, they act as a specialist that blends insider and outsider knowledge to offer their clients something that no staff member can provide. If, however, you're a management, business or communications consultant – i.e. not the medical kind – prepare to be referred to as 'the type that doesn't help people'. And maybe that fundamental misnomer is where we need to begin.

I've had a lot of experience around consultants. I am one, I work a lot with others. I've been managed by them, reported to them, or had them report to me. Depending on your experience with consultants, if it's anything like mine, you've dealt with characters that ranged from guns for hire, to data nerds, to shot callers, to pen pushers, to fat cats, to some prick with an MBA and an opinion. If we're really honest, they can often be loathsome, commitaphobes, let loose from a clusterfuck corral of type-A personalities, in chosen a career that allows them to dip-in and dip-out of departments, companies, geographies and responsibilities – ever careful to avoid getting too close for comfort.

In their defence, consultants must straddle polar-opposite roles, sitting somewhere between an unrecognizable outsider and a trusted expert advisor to the highest levels of an organization, but it's often in a manner that closer resembles manspreading. It can be overbearing, overdressed and altogether too invasive. Understandably, this can give the rest of us a bad rep.

The manner in which so many consultants don't get on with people offers a baffling snapshot of a relationship-based profession. If you have hired them, they're not like any other staff you have, for better or for worse. They're not "all in" on your dream, because they're half in by design. You may spend more of your time thinking about their motives, qualifications, or capability than the organizational issue you hired them to address. They have their own employer, their own career objectives, even their own industry – one worth over $250 billion globally to boot.

But good consultants, the type we all want to hire, learn from or even be, are an entirely different proposition. These ones are worth their weight in gold.

Like gold, consultancy is only valuable under the right conditions; when understood in the right ways. From a consultant's perspective, we are an outsider working on room-and-board basis and our impact is judged on the results we delivered. Or, in the case of one project I worked on, we were boardroom captives, lucky if water and WiFi were allowed that day. In many ways, there can be a lack of control that comes to define your career. Due to any number of different personality traits in a room, this lack of control quickly manifests as tension – an ever-present feeling that a misplaced HDMI adaptor can start a gnawing creep from the CEO's side towards an often-helpless hired help. More distressingly, this lack of control can be the death knell of a project – the wall between you and the results you are being paid to deliver.

If you regularly find yourself questioning the value of your existence in this role (even half as often as I do), look no further than the consultant-playing role of the world's leading military advisors for some reasonably sordid solace and know you are not alone.

U.S armed forced have provided equipment, training and on-going advisory support – that is to say, "consultancy" – to more than three-quarters of the known world.

The latest figures suggest that US Military personnel deliver IMET (International Military Education and Training) under the banner of 'military aid' in most of the 150 countries in which they have a presence. And while it may seem a world away from the glass-cased offices you find yourself in today, IMET is essentially a consultancy offering, delivering operational development, infrastructure support, and on-going advisory. In the express goals of the U.S. State Department, this is aligned under a simple heading of 'self-sufficiency'.

The focus then is to train the future trainers and specialist operators so they may train their peers and work autonomously.

Outside of the US, China, Russia and a handful of others, many countries lack the manpower, experience or the educational acumen to develop their own training programs.

There is nothing inherently unique or different about this, and its application to communications consultancy is certainly no different. As a key component of project oversight in any type of consultancy, on-going training and operational support ensures that the expert advisors can continue to guide those who have hired them until everyone in the organization is completely satisfied in their own ability to execute alone.

Whether in corporate speak or military training, this type of approach is called BOT. Disappointingly not referring to a helpful robot butler, BOT stands for 'Build, Operate, Transfer'. The consultants design and develop an appropriate working infrastructure with proven working processes (Build); hire and support a functioning team to meet the organisational need in question (Operate); and train the internal staff to the point where the expert consultants are no longer needed (Transfer). Sounds straightforward enough, right? If only.

The challenge, as you may have already guessed, is the often-polarizing view of what defines 'self-sufficient'. I've found this to be even more of an issue when hierarchy, cultural differences, and ego (usually a shit-ton of ego) come into play. One man's trash is another man's treasure, or so the saying goes. The success of any BOT project hinges on the ability to handover, but just when handover comes is wildly open to interpretation.

For example, would you say that the self-sufficiency phase is complete with the teams' ability to do something you have taught them, or should it only be the ability to do it near flawlessly, successfully and consistently? Or somewhere in between?

When time is money and appearing to understand is a safer career move than admitting you don't, the consultants' ability to deliver becomes an inherently human affair with severe commercial consequences. To succeed then, you must be a mentor, motivator and even manipulator, as you try to tiptoe the eggshell-laden path to project completion, client contentment, and even commercial fulfilment. How's that for a wanky way to describe a job well done?

Let's take our example further and look at client-consultant tension in the US-Military backed Middle Eastern Gulf and North Africa – namely in the case of those who've worked with the Egyptians. And while I had my own list of insurmountable frustrations, cultural roadblocks, and facepalm emojis while consulting across this region, there is nothing quite as telling, or potentially disastrous, as the outcomes of bad military client relationships. Unlike the more familiar row over the opening of a CEO speech, the target of a tweet, or the headline of an article you tried to place, this kind of advisor-stonewalling has resulted in catastrophic events, civilian death and untold destruction on more than one occasion.

Since the delivery of Lockheed F-16s to the Egyptian Air Force (EAF) in 2000, the United States Air Force (USAF) has been providing extensive military advisory and support. Just like the aftersales services and support you expect when buying a new car, the USAF provide help and guidance to those it equips with multirole fighter aircraft. Despite this on-going assistance from one of the world's leading air forces, the EAF continually rank highest amongst F-16 damage and destruction reports held by supplier Lockheed Martin. The reason? Well, believe it or not, the Egyptian military, unfortunately, never seem to listen. Sound familiar?

Expert sources continually site the EAF's standard pattern of attack as a cause for critical operational failure. Yes – you read that correctly, the *standard* pattern of attack causes critical failure. One where two fighter jets approach nearly simultaneously from either side of a target, on a collision course. One where the best-case scenario is that the pilots swerve to avoid collision and the manoeuvre "makes any attempt to target accurately unfeasible". And when the expert Air Force strategists say a defence strategy is 'unfeasible', they're kindly saying it's as sensible as chopping off your fingers to avoid the off chance you might one day catch them in a door.

Worse still, the same insiders report that the Egyptians were not recording their missions or holding debriefing sessions, let alone actually evaluating their own performances. Whether rooted in an organizational culture where authority is feared, or a professional air of infallibility, these practices have become highly detrimental institutionalized elements of EAF training. American pilots have reported constant frustration trying to convince the EAF that its school solutions are not only wrong, but potentially fatal. One USAF pilot who trained the EAF reported to author and analyst, Kenneth Pollock, that it was "probably good" that the Egyptians didn't use live ordnance in practice. If they did, they would lose a lot more of their aircraft and pilots to these ridiculous tactics – before they even made it as far as facing an enemy.

Before we have a look at the learning at play here, it's as important to note that the US military experts are not alone in the Middle Eastern melting pots of malpractice. Pollock also explains that the Russians had near identical experiences. For instance, in the run-up to the October War of 1973, the Egyptians adopted Soviet tactics to a greater extent than ever before. In an exploitation of their military might and strategic thinking at the time, Soviet combat doctrine was to have the commander of a tank platoon designate a single target, at which the entire platoon (three tanks, including the commander's) would fire until it was destroyed. At that point, the commander would designate a new target. The Soviets calculated that, given the gunnery skills of their crews, it normally would take three salvos from the platoon (or nine shots) to kill an enemy tank. In any context, this is excellent use of insight-driven efficiencies in business, or war. However, rather than see this as a general guide for planning, the Egyptians turned it into a hard-and-fast rule and taught all of their tank platoons to fire three salvos at the designated target and then move on to the next target. Better safe than sorry, was the intention. The reality was closer to what you might find in a Monty Python sketch.

Egyptian tank gunnery turned out to be, well, pretty shit in comparison to their Soviet counterparts. As a result, during the October War, it was often the case that none of the shots fired in the three salvos of an Egyptian tank platoon assault would hit the Israeli tank it had targeted. Nevertheless, because the Egyptians had been taught to fire three salvos and then move on, they would shift their fire to the next target even though they had not actually destroyed the first one. The outcome was three-fold – firstly, a lot of relieved Israeli tank platoons; secondly, a lot of lost Egyptian tank platoons during tank duels; and thirdly, a lot of Russian military advisors driven to despair.

These examples, extreme or not, typify the paradox of life as a client advisor. Hired for your expertise but retained for your impact – often while kept at arms-length from the decisions and actions that have the greatest effect and chance of you delivering the results you're being paid for. The reality is that there will always be a gap between the expertise we have and the expertise we can give. Sometimes it can be lost in misunderstanding, while other times it can be blocked by egos or sheer ignorance.

As it was best described to me, there are those who give advice and those whose advice is sought – and the two are more mutually exclusive than many would think. Whether hired as a media advisor, wedding planner or military strategist – however brilliant – there's little chance of success unless we first convince the people involved to allow us to do what success entails.

People, as we'll explore throughout this book, are the only pathways to success, or the barriers to entry, within our environment. Their trust has to be cultivated, coerced and championed so they can feel like our solutions, however offered, were first sought. Their personalities, moods and whims must be navigated, and their often-ill-advised tangents temporarily indulged. It has to make sense, rather than just *be sensible*. It's an undeniably funny thing we do, consulting. There's no denying it. We are psychologists, sociologists, best friends, older siblings, agony aunts, silent partners, vocal advocates, drinking buddies, mentors, mentees, guidance counsellors and chaperons to anyone we work for.

Understanding the people who hire us, earning their trust, and convincing them that our advice is valuable, is central to who we are, so that we can do what we do. The road to success as a consultant can only be taken hand in hand – commitment issues sold separately...

CHAPTER THREE

A FISHERMAN'S TALE

"Teach a man to fish; you feed him for a lifetime"

- Lao Tzu

We are what we repeatedly do, Will Durant said of excellence. And what we repeatedly and, endlessly do as humans is communicate. From subtle, subconscious ticks to extravagant exclamations, our world and our environment is defined by the millions of means for imparting information. Communicating exceptionally, and effectively, on behalf of anyone, to anyone else, is an entirely different proposition.

For many people, the distinction between personal and professional communications is clearly defined by the latter's use of tools and tacit tactics to promote a commercially motivated point of view. This, however, may be further from the truth than we expect. There may even be more similarities than we ever could have imagined. In this purpose-defining chapter, we draw the lines and then connect the dots between the characteristics of innate human communication, and the role of dedicated communications professionals.

First things first, let's look back at the people who came before the profession and the important lessons of our exceptionally social species' early development.

Starting our journey in nomadic tribes, then small settlements, then villages, then kingdoms, then cities, then nations, and now citizens of the world, the survival and success of our kind is indisputably thanks to that comparably oversized, incredibly complex organ between our ears. The brain has allowed us to communicate, organize, outthink and outmanoeuvre almost any living thing that tries to get in our way. Survival amongst humans has always hinged on our ability to understand, navigate and progress within social structures and interpersonal relationships. Failure to do so is death, and literally was for most of our known history.

Hopefully by now, you don't face a fatal outcome for the words that fall from your lips, but you may need to consider such extremes for your business. Professional, commercial and political crisis have never been a more common killer of dreams, deals and livelihoods. It has also given rise to the ever-expansive function of "Communications" we represent.

Despite these seemingly humble and insular beginnings, every human alive today engages in at least one officially recognized language, and 85% of people can now understand written communication – with literacy rates consistently up from a lowly 12% in the Industrial Age, just 200 years ago. Not a bad jump for just 1% of the existence of our species, right? Check us out – quite the communicators.

The problem is that the more complex, interconnected and global our not-so little worlds have become, the more we're finding that the communications skills, customs and norms that got us through the last 199,980 years have struggled to keep up with the last 20. If you work in the communications profession, it's enough to keep you awake at night.

In this decade of hyperconnected, integrated, information overload, why does it feel more difficult than ever to communicate truthfully, effectively and meaningfully? Why do we *still* suffer misunderstanding? How are so many of us so bad at one of the most basic functions of our existence? One reason, as we've established, is that we're all overwhelmed. There is too much communication, too many forms, and too many mediums – it's too many signals, too little time. You could say that there have never been so many ways to fail.

Let's say that you can read and speak English, for example. Did you know that there are a possible 171,476 words to get to grips with? But '*words*'? Nobody writes those anymore. Better to find one of the 3,000 emojis that have made their way from the tweets of tweens to the ink-stained fingertips of global political leaders. But wait – what if they don't interpret emojis the same way as you do? Is that a grin or a grimace? Is heart-eyes too much? Will they know I'm being sarcastic? Actually, should you just try and find a GIF? Or maybe a dog meme? What if they're a cat person? Feeling overwhelmed yet? Me too.

'*Teach a man to fish; you feed him for a lifetime*", or so the saying goes. Well, in today's interconnected world of communication (and emojification), Chinese philosopher Lao Tzu's proverb needs an addendum, especially for those working across the exceptionally diversified field of communications: teach a man to fish and you *may* feed him for a lifetime, but that definitely doesn't make him a fisherman. Indeed, it is the gap between our ability to communicate, and the competency, flexibility and consistency required of an exceptional communications professional, that we have to try and fill.

One individual who leaves no doubt as to their professional mastery, international impact and ideologically-defined purpose in communications is a man called Roger Stone – even if he does use his powers for evil. He is a terrifying, best-in-class case study for how to achieve the effective, meaningful communication – the kind that truly connects speaker with audience, in a way that so many today can only dream of.

Roger Stone, if you haven't come across the name before, is widely regarded as the master manipulator who exploited the economic, social and political conditions that saw Donald Trump elected to the White House. According to his own biography, Roger (as Trump calls him) is a seasoned political operative, speaker, pundit, and New York Times Bestselling Author, also featured in the must-watch Netflix documentary "Get me Roger

Stone". His role in political communications began in the state-shaking scandal of Watergate, and it seems the taste for blood hasn't left his lips since.

When it comes to the high-seas metaphor for professional communications, Roger Stone is part Somali-pirate, part Cold-War submarine, and part the greatest fisherman to ever sail the seas. By leveraging his exceptional understanding of mass communications for   political point-scoring, power-retention, and pure, unfiltered divisiveness, Stone probably read Lao Tzu and thought, "Why feed the village when you can keep the fish, blame someone else for the widespread starvation, and watch the madness unfold."

There's something frighteningly vivid about spitefully purposeful people – talent, traits and tools deliberately misused for malicious means. A bit like Scar in Disney's *Lion King*, determined to seize Mufasa's throne by any means necessary. Through this lens, we can say that Stone's talent is epitomized in the use of country-dividing rhetoric, underhand tactics, and deep, unrelenting bellows within favourable echo chambers – often in a confrontational way that has come to define his modus operandi and his raison d'etre. Stone, you see, is a human pendulum that swings between two points – contrarian and anarchist. He knows it, and now we know it; and his rise has been perfectly timed to poke, prod and provoke an increasingly aggravated audience. However-aggrieved at the success of his practice, we all can learn something from the intensely well-informed, highly experienced approach.

Roger Stone not only crafted the Trump presidential rise, but interestingly did so by curation as much as conflation.

With decades of experience canvassing and operating in the frontlines of the US Republican party, Stone evolved from a finger on the pulse to the throbbing artery of the red side of the aisle. This role gave him unrivalled perspective on the hopes, fears and ambitions of the masses – especially the dark, dirty-laundry revelations usually hushed in whispered voices or reserved for behind closed doors. By utilizing established relationship and stakeholder networks that track from Republican leaders like Reagan, Nixon and Trump, through the Republican membership echo chambers of Fox News, Breitbart, and InfoWars, Stone made the most of his standing at the epicentre of an information database that drove, irked, outraged and emboldened US Republicans. The man was a walking match, with a lifetime dedicated to gathering the gasoline.

The rest, as we know, is civil-liberty-crushing history for the United States of America, and so many of its counterparts around the world. With Roger Stone's coined term, "Fake News", on the lips of every politician and toddler who sees something they don't like, the communication landscape changes immeasurably forever. That is the legacy of the archetypical master of perception and persuasion. And I know that's a harrowing thought. More harrowing still, is the shocking realization that someone as despicable and mean-spirited as Roger Stone, is also the perfect segue to 'empathy'.

Think about it.

Success in communications consultancy is essentially about helping people to understand a point of view; and it is achieved in any circumstances, by any terms, as an approach – for better or for worse. If Denzel Washington is The Equalizer, then our goal is to be *The Empathizer*. And rather than the limp-wristed agony-aunt you might imagine, empathizers are also forces to be reckoned with.

Empathy is one of the most misinterpreted characteristics of our time. Synonymous with weakness, concession and even sympathy, empathy actually refers to nothing of the sort. Empathy understood correctly is, as we said, a tool: the ability to understand others, to take on their perspective of the world. Whether that tool is engaged and applied personally, professionally or philosophically is up to you, but having it at your disposal sets the foundation for everything that follows.

Empathizers also make the best communicators not only because we're very good at reading people, but because we can be quite self-assured in knowing what success feels like. We know that it doesn't need a *Cannes Lion* award, a handshake from the boss, or even a thank you from the client. What I have learned, more than anything, is that the pride is in the outcome, regardless of the means. Successful communicators have to be the empathy-espousing career fishermen and women who consistently feed the village, by committing to understanding the villagers' needs.

The most valuable thing that I have learned from almost a decade of study, practice, and personal and professional growth in this industry is that there's a knack to learning that just isn't hackable. It's a blend that's concocted in terms of hours of discipline, dedication, solitude, frustration, despair and enlightenment. It's endless; and has to be seen that way if we're going to keep up with the pace of change around us. And yet, you can only go through that once you're at least beginning to come to terms with your "Why". Well, before Roger Stone found his (highly questionable) "Why", one French philosopher was asking, "Why we why" in the first place.

You may have come across René Descartes' "I think, therefore I am" before now. Maybe you referenced the 'Father of Modern Philosophy' in a college assignment you tried to sound learned in. You may even have been so bold as to refer to its originally published French version, "Je pense, donc je suis", or the widely cited Latin iteration, "Cogito, ergo sum" – you old sage, you. The meaning of the phrase is, however, often lost in translation. In his ground-breaking 17th Century writings, Descartes defined human nature by our very ability to think existentially. That we can think about, consider and interrogate our existence, and indeed our thoughts, is what makes us human. René Descartes did not, in contrast, intend to provide a seemingly intellectual, fill-in-the-blanks-as-you-see-fit-catch-all for professional self-identification. I think like a communicator, therefore, I am a communicator. Not on my watch. And it is the over-complication of Descartes very simple maxim that most commonly defines the world we live in today.

As a philosopher, mathematician and scientist, Descartes pondered, explored and interrogated some of the most complex intellectual challenges of his then-modern time. The man is credited with inventing (if that's the word) analytical geometry – a bridge between algebra and geometry. What I respect and admire most of Descartes, having only an ignorant understanding of his accomplishments, is his incredible ability to identify, codify and simplify.

This is the very essence of our role as communications professionals.

It's the very reason why we are and must continue to be incessant researchers, endless learners and unassuming interrogators. We do the work, the exploring, the failing, the finding, the testing, so that the end result can be the most engaging, impactful and simple idea that we can humanly provide. The world that we live in is too complex to allow anything less.

Our work is full to the brim of backseat drivers, keyboard warriors and armchair experts. In fact, we're being drowned out and often overthrown by them. The people who, if you cured cancer, would blame you for not doing so sooner, or quicker, or easier, or cheaper. Nothing was ever achieved on intent, and even less by contempt. When understanding your role and function as the communications professional, it's better to pay attention to Theodore "Teddy" Roosevelt than the office parasite, who only has cynical "whys" to undermine your efforts to think and do differently. In an excerpt from a speech delivered in Paris, on April 23rd, 1910, Roosevelt said:

"It is not the critic who counts; not the man who points out how the strong man stumbles, or where the doer of deeds could have done them better. The credit belongs to the man who is actually in the arena, whose face is marred by dust and sweat and blood; who strives valiantly; who errs, who comes short again and again, because there is no effort without error and shortcoming; but who does actually strive to do the deeds; who knows great enthusiasms, the great devotions; who spends himself in a worthy cause; who at the best knows in the end the triumph of high achievement, and who at the worst, if he fails, at least fails while daring greatly, so that his place shall never be with those cold and timid souls who neither know victory nor defeat."

It is not an overstatement to stress that everyone who wants to succeed in communications has to figure out, and more consciously decide, what type of operator they want to be: the motivator, the anarchist, the thinker, the doer, the planner, the creative, the workhorse, the fixer, the team player, the solo-runner, the all-nighter, the early-riser, the superstar, the recluse, the all-rounder. Importantly though, none of these descriptions refer to specific functions or aspects of communications work. I don't want you to decide to be the media expert, the digital guru or the client confidante. Between the timeless greats I have studied and the contemporary trailblazers I've had the pleasure of working with, I can truly say that this career is fundamentally about your character. Your attitude. How you choose to conduct yourself, and what you choose to represent.

After all, how can you advise clients about how to define themselves, if you haven't even managed it of yourself?

The time will always come, early in your career, when it is your character, not your technical skills, that will be tested. It may even be found wanting. That's OK too. Whether intrinsically, intellectually or financially motivated, there is a way to go about your business that ensures longevity and success in any type of consultancy, not least the communications industry.

For us, the brave and the faithful (or inexplicably enthusiastic and undoubtedly under-resourced), the heart of motivation has to be some sort of fascination with people – what they think, why they think it, and how we might change or reinforce that thinking – how we convey what we mean and, in turn, make them able to understand. After all, human beings have interacted, connected and divided for all of time, at unimaginable scale, by incredibly diverse means. With all of this hinging on the communication of needs, wants and ideas, how fun would it be to get involved?

CHAPTER FOUR

MEAN(ING) MACHINE

"What do you mean?"

- Justin Bieber

In 2015, pop superstar Justin Bieber sang, *"When you nod your head yes, but you wanna say, no – What do you mean?"* and I felt that. We all did. Because, after years of trial and error in trying to communicate and to understand all that happens arounds us, we soon come to a realisation that it's an incredibly difficult thing to do – to create and share meaning. And yet, it's more important and challenging than ever in the work we do.

In this chapter – one that took more scribbles, rewrites and sleepless nights than any other – we have to strip back from the talk and tactics to explore the critical role of meaning, in all its forms. By championing some innovative communications thinkers that faced this tricky topic head on, and in managing to go from Bieber to Bananarama, we'll try to wrap our heads around the mind-boggling mapping of meaning. The good news is that it's probably something you've always done.

****

Famous inventors always seem to be described as insatiably curious technophiles – and no, that's not the type you find French-kissing a USB port. From Edison to Dyson to Ford, those who used their minds to change the world were invariably born with a will to think differently, and a knack to turn their hand to mechanical and electrical engineering. In what is now Disney-defined cliché, an inventor's childhood is immortalised in soft-focus montages of intellectual exploration – treasure hunts, nut-and-bolt-strewn toolboxes, electrical wiring, sticky-note scribbles, and a halo-glow from a computer screen. Fair or not, most of our understanding of what it means to be an innovator is rooted in a tactile understanding of innovation and invention. Although the definition of invention broadly refers to processes and ideas, what we all picture are 'real' inventions. You know, the kind your parents would name –tactile, mechanical, digital. Things.

So, what of those whose talent is less tangible? Those, for whom the innovation has no off-switch, screen, handle, or line of code?

For me, the tireless pulling-apart and rebuilding of things was there for as long as I can remember – it just took place within the circuits and hardware of my little noggin. I lay awake at night, among the glow-in-the-dark sticky-ceiling-stars, exploring ideas, sayings and conversations; flipping them around, turning them inside out, all the while trying to understand how and why different people had different reaction to them. I still do – minus the glow-in-the dark stars. Now, after 20-odd years of playing with meaning, my internal database of references, symbols and perspectives has grown to a level that sparks, rewires and connects day and night, 365 days a year. It gives you an awareness of the power of words and symbols you never thought possible, and with that, the ability to catch words that trip from your tongue, as you constantly monitor the give-and-take of conversation at any level of scale.

On the theoretical side, the study of meaning falls under two main camps – semantics and semiotics. Both are important in the multimedia-content cacophony that surrounds us today. So, let's take a look at them one by one.

Semantics is derived from the Greek word for significance and is the study of linguistic meaning. Despite humble beginnings in tightly knit human tribes, the constant evolution and homogenisation of spoken and written language makes the mastery of semantics an increasingly difficult thing, not least for international consultants, marketeers and branding experts. If you're ever in doubt, there's always one great example to prove the rule. According to marketing folklore, one of the most famous examples of a linguistic faux pas for the English-speaking regions of the globe is attributed to Colgate, one of the top oral hygiene brands in the world. While we may know it as a trusted sink-side companion to keep our pearly-whites pearly and white, it turns out that in Spanish speaking-countries, it roughly translates to 'hang yourself' (Cuel-Ga-Teh). Eh, que? Granted, that's an extreme example, but the pitfalls of linguistic inconsideration are far more problematic than we may have appreciated. Consequently, appreciating language, meaning, and understanding are far more important than you may think.

For most of us, the problems are more minor than suicide encouragement from our toothpaste. We all fall foul of the most basic misinterpretations, missteps and malpractice in our use of words. Men, it seems, far more so than women.

They say 93% of communication is non-verbal. Well, anyone with an ounce of awareness will know that the female race has long known the difference between what is said, how it is said, and what is actually meant; not least when compared to their male counterparts. "I'm fine" is the long-holding precedence in this case. Allow me to generalise for a moment... Us literal, linguistic philistines of the male species tend to take words on their face value: "I am fine" pertaining to a state of satisfactory disposition. Our more advanced female counterparts, on the other hand, dance with the devil in the details of delivery. Be the words uttered, mumbled or delivered with the fervour of the recently converted, the female "I'm fine" can be loaded with the mood-killing capabilities of a steel-toe kick to the gonads, despite what it says on the tin. Women, then, suffer with our ignorance, and men, down tools on proverbial bridge-building. Everyone loses as a result.

This breakdown in communication in our personal lives leaves us red-faced and despaired; professionally, however, we cannot allow it. So, whether you're fine, grand, good, or great, awareness of semantics is a critical tool to relationship building and client management, especially for anyone in communications. Complicated as it is, however, we similarly have semiotics to contend with.

Semiotics, on the other side, is the study of signs and symbols. It includes everything from hand signals, like 'thumbs up', to emojis, like... 'thumbs up'. In a trend that pre-dates 6,000-year-old ancient Egyptian hieroglyphics, it includes any non-word form that has a shared human interpretation. Today, more than ever, it is an amazing amassment of content and codification, regularly contributing to miscommunication.

Symbols, you see, are short-hand for incredibly complex sets of ideological beliefs – each with the potential to be adopted under a reimagined interpretation for a specific individual or group. Historically, a cross, or crescent moon, for example have proven enough to unite and divide billions of people across the world. And today, fraught debate rages as to whether the internationally understood "OK" hand-gesture has been hijacked by white supremacists. Understanding the constantly evolving significance and sensitivities of symbolism, then, is critical to ensure unintentional and unforgiveable lines are never crossed.

A picture may say a thousand words, but many of those words may not be as obvious or important to your audiences as they are for you – likewise, they may be more cherished and revered than you ever expected. Through a reliance on implicity of meaning (the assumption that a symbol or image will relay the exact meaning you intend it to for anyone who sees it), semiotics has the ability to build or break brands. Using it, then, should come with a warning sign.

Combined, semiotics and semantics form the foundation for the entire field of social science – the field that our profession lives off. Psychology, sociology, anthropology, political science and even economics are anchored in a commitment to identify, understand and dissect the spheres of shared meaning and misunderstanding between people. Great communicators, the ones worth learning from, are the architects, interior designers, landscapers and painter-decorators of much of what developed from these foundations.

****

We have more words and symbols to think about than ever before, and more channels, platforms and means of distribution than ever, but like an hour scrolling on Netflix or a child who panic-chooses vanilla ice-cream, being spoiled for choice is not always a good thing.

Meaning, it seems, is (*almost*) more important than anything else. Without it, we're just exhausting ourselves with noisemaking; and without mastering it, we're multi-channel mistake-makers. Extreme, I know, but let's keep it in mind as we strive to really think hard about what we do, and what we have to offer the world. In bringing the theory to practice then, we accept that in order to engage audiences – to truly engage them, for their benefit and ours – our approach is defined by the mantra that, "meaning justifies the means", if you will. This is a beautiful marriage between the 'why' of our clients and organisations' communications – the meaning they would like their audience to understand and engage with – and the 'how' to support it – the means. While this may be a new and exciting perspective for many of us today, it turns out there was a Canadian man who figured it out over fifty years ago.

Herbert Marshall McLuhan (1911 – 1980), of Edmonton, Canada, has the enviable distinction of being defined as a philosopher, futurist and communications theorist. He is the poster boy of communications academia, if almost entirely unknown in the outside world. In one of the most well informed and earliest predictions of globalisation, he referred to a future "global village", defined by a new form of global collectivism which is shaped by the expanding prevalence and penetration of technology in defining our lives and social norms. Basically, he foresaw the technology-supported impact of shared global identity, and a dilution of truly local culture. McLuhan was putting this detailed prediction in books and academic papers in 1960, meanwhile your local weatherman still can't predict if you should bring a jacket to work tomorrow. What a man. For his part, McLuhan earned this reputation through a combination of exceptional vision, pragmatic theorisation, and disciplined interrogation of the world around us. For our part, he made an assertion about meaning that has yet to be surpassed.

McLuhan's focus on communications delivery has defined the foundations for almost every communications industry professional in existence. His view of organisational interaction, and the role of trained professionals in deciding and deciphering them, makes him the architect of modern communications specialisation. He is the one to draw the lines for an industry that has grown to an estimated global value in the multi-millions, without many within it ever hearing of his name.

McLuhan's simple dictum, "the medium is the message" managed to articulate the role of the 'how' in conveying meaning, and it remains to this day the greatest, most overlooked insight in modern communications practice. For the simplest interpretation I can think of, McLuhan was pre-emptively beating Bananarama and The Fun Boy Three to, "It ain't what you do, it's the way that you do it". What McLuhan has added to this catchy 80s hook is that *how* you do something in our endlessly diversifying world of communications, sets both the rules and impact of whatever you are trying to say.

A tweet carries with it an implication of accessibility and brevity – it's most often a broadcast about a moment in time, aimed at nobody in particular. A signed letter evokes a sense of formality – the weight of who signed it, and what logo is on the letterhead, most likely as important if not more important than its contents. A photocall needs to be visually led, honed by a photographer's eye, and for the love of God delivered without a cardboard cut-out of a hashtag. A press conference, as you might imagine, should suggest timeliness and newsworthiness – a reason to gather time-starved journalists from the plethora of potential leads at their desks; and something that gains significance by how it is delivered, and by whom. A speech should be audience appropriate, representative of the organisation behind the person speaking, and timed correctly to ensure it doesn't affect other speakers who may have to follow. Simple or obvious as all of that seems, you may or may not be surprised how many people in the industry need to print that paragraph and stick it on their desks!

I've been there – for all of the above, in all their shame and glory. From hours and hours on op-eds that were never (ever) going to be acceptable for earned media, to the biggest cardboard cut-outs of letters nobody gave a shit about, there are things we all have to do as we cut our teeth as consultants. We're in the trenches, obsessing over content – words, images, slogans and hashtags – every day for years on end, and it becomes all too easy and all too forgivable to spend very little time interrogating how best to share it with the world. The fact remains that the communication of meaning is an all-encompassing process, with each element requiring the same care and attention you need when you're anxious or hungover – yeah, that much.

From boardrooms to billboards, the curse of crippling, over-thought, over-written content delivered the wrong way has undone well-meaning interns, seasoned politicians, and multinational CEOs alike. It's a Truman Show-esque belief that *everything* we say matters, but we can't help it. Like a five-year-old with a secret, the act of knowing everything that we now know is not enough for contentment. If anything, all this information about sharing information is a burden.

So, here and now, we should take a stand.

If we let a client speak without something to say, sign a letter that ought to have been a tweet, or gather journalists with nothing to offer, we let the client and ourselves down. If we allow that, we've missed the biggest trick in communications – impact. How then, do we know when we can achieve this?

As we have established, meaning only really exists when it is shared. It therefore requires awareness of the passive, oxygen-like omnipotence of meaning in our everyday lives, and the ability to turn our hand to using it for high-involvement interaction. Endless give and take. Success in our world, then, lives and breathes for those who are capable of speaking to people on their terms, in their field of play. It can be fluent, fluid or an old-fashioned 'fuck you'; a tweet, a TedTalk or a text message; there are no points for trying, nor medals for taking part in this cutthroat, outcomes-focused business that is engagement and influence. For Trump, it's a CAPS LOCK, cat-calling Twitter rant to his disenfranchised, #MAGA-mania supporters, for Dove it's a soft-spoken, inclusive, female voice that speaks to everyone and anyone, and for you it might be the tea-sipping DMC (deep meaningful conversation) you have with your best friend going through a rough patch. In the end, there's a way to communicate with people that is appropriate and impactful. There's tact, and tone, and timing all tied into the

83

delivery of meaning, and we have the fortune of being responsible for all of it.

Your job, should you be called upon, is the ability to deliver any and all of the examples above in a measured way. Granting myself permission to finish with a recklessly over-indulgent term, "meaning" is the quintessence of the communications profession itself.

Now, with our quintessence in hand, it's off to see what we need to do with it.

CHAPTER FIVE

RELATIONSHIP GOALS

"Service to others is the rent you pay for your room here on earth"

- Mohammad Ali

Mohammad Ali was right when he described service to others as the "rent you pay for your time here on earth". What we can now safely add is that the property market of life is crashing, rental prices are soaring and the only room you can afford for all your hard work is a shithole, probably advertised as "quaint". Welcome to the endless hours, thankless tasks, and pointless PowerPoints of consultancy services.

Don't worry, it's not all doom and gloom – at least not all doom and gloom all of the time. No matter where you are, who your clients are, or what your job title, you essentially have relationships to focus on. Like any relationship you have in your life, from your mother to your barber, the client relationships you can be proud of are entirely based in understanding and mutual respect. Unlike your mother, in this case, time is often defined by money.

Money talks. But no advisor should talk for money. The value proposition to any advisor worth their 'billables' is the relationship itself. It is a living, breathing, mortality-defined thing that needs to be treated that way. It requires conception, creation, building, nourishment and sustenance, for as long as it can possibly be beneficial to both parties and their common goal. For that to happen, like in any other relationship we can think of, there has to be flexibility on both sides.

When we are hired as a perceived non-essential resource, it helps on our side of things to have the flexibility of a Chinese gymnast at the Beijing Olympics. So, without a criminally abusive coach and medieval style torture devices, how do we stretch to the changing demands, personalities, and expectations that every new project brings? For the communicator in us, flexibility hinges on the singular idea of understanding – yourself, others, context, sticking points, no-go areas, acceptable compromises, mutual benefits. How exactly to identify, navigate, and surmount these elements requires looking at things a little differently. I've somehow come to see it as a cocktail concoction of marriage, crocodiles, camels, and judo. Bear with me.

Outside of infidelity, Marriage.com consistently reports that money stress and lack of communication are the ever-competing runners-up in the reasons why couples seek counselling or divorce. If you're a consultant who advises or operates across multiple projects and clients, you already get a free pass on that first one – not a bad start, by all accounts – but the other reasons should seem very familiar indeed. More interesting still is that constant arguing, and unrealistic expectations incessantly round out the top five malignant tumours of matrimony. Undoubtedly, for our purposes, four of the top five issues are based in communications. As someone who has never been married, and therefore never divorced, all I know is that all four of these are the biggest issues consultants face in the entirely inescapable, increasingly inseparable role of client management.

In fact, the term "client management" is the most obvious place to start. It's one of those descriptions that have always been there, but once you stop to think about it, you realize how fucked up it is – you know, like finding out for the first time that the Kardashians exist, and never being able to live in ignorant bliss again. It automatically frames the relationship in the terms more appropriate for a lion-tamer, snake charmer, or child-minder. One side is in charge of keeping the other in check – for "their own benefit", of course. Whether starting out in consultancy, or a veteran client manager, you will soon know that "relationship management" is a far more appropriate term. As the service provider, the internal-external inbetweener, the goal for you should be nothing less than symbiosis.

Symbiotic relations hinge on interaction between two different organisms living in close physical association, where both can survive off each other. Back in my days of school, there was only one kind of symbiosis – the kind where everyone is happier for the relationship. Now, it turns out there's actually a few. The bad kind of symbiosis is parasitic relationships and, needless to say, this is the 'how to lose clients and influence nobody' approach. The good kind we need to think about is called mutualism. Rather than the name of a California-based Netflix documentary, mutualism refers *mutually beneficial* relationships in which both sides are better for having the other. So, while bees and flowers might be the most obvious example, the crocodile and the bird might just be the best example of mutualism on the planet. The heroes we need, if maybe not the ones we want, if Christopher Nolan ever had anything to do with it.

Long before consultants were suiting-up for the benefit of their boardroom-based billable-buyers, one of the oldest creatures on the planet had teamed up with an unlikely friend: this is the story of Nile crocodiles and Egyptian plover birds. The crocodiles, unsurprisingly, are carnivores. Not unlike that overeager friend of yours in a nightclub, their only criteria for something to chase is that it represents a living organism. In the case of Nile crocodiles, and not your friend Niall whose been single for four years, that means birds, frogs, fish and anything else that wanders a little too close to the water's edge. Anything, that is, with one very particular exception – a distinctively feathered, 20cm long, Egyptian plover bird. The reason? Simple. The Nile crocodile doesn't have a toothbrush, and tooth decay is a bitch. The service that follows is a thing of beauty.

After a hard-won meal, ripped from the embankment without so much as a moment to reflect on the life they were leaving behind, the shredded carcass, ligament and muscle of the prey causes a bit of posthumous niggle to our predatory protagonist. "What's a croc to do?" You might ask. Well, it all starts with a very simple signal. In what may appear to be some sort of prey-baiting tactic, the crocodile lies deathly still with an open mouth... Only this time, it means they are ready to be serviced. Like that person in the office whose email inbox is immaculately filed, the plover bird gets straight to work, flying right in to the world's most hostile working environment. There, they to begin pecking and picking at the food scraps around the crocodile's teeth. Clean teeth, full bird, can't lose.

Now, I don't know what motivated the first suicidal plover bird to choose this precarious dining table, but the reality is that the setup has benefited both bird and croc for many hundreds of years. Something we as an industry can only aspire to.

If you're still scratching your head at the use of crocodile teeth-cleaning instead of the tried and trusted story of bees and pollen, the deliberate act of those involved in our example offers far clearer a learning – one which can be broken down into three central elements.

The first step is problem identification – the most impactful, valuable work is necessary for clients because it addresses a fundamental problem or challenge that, without you, the external resource, they couldn't figure out. Once identified, the next step is to devise a solution that is both understood and agreeable for the client – as we learned from the Mild-Mannered Mercenaries, it's no good having a solution if the client won't accept it. Finally, and most obviously, deliver on that commitment – which actually refers less to execution skill, and more to a shared understanding of what success looks like. In summary it's problem + solution + execution = impact.

Perhaps the strangest thing you might have noticed about this example – and, admittedly, there are plenty of strange things within it – is that we don't pay much attention to how the plover bird goes about their business. And this is interesting, because it breaks down most of the assumptions we hold, and flies in the face of the advice shared by every YouTube ad pushy sales guru. Fundamentally, it actually doesn't matter how charming or funny or kind or helpful or intelligent you are. Clients really care about what they are paying you to fix. Sure, the other stuff helps at the beginning, and is a great tool to rely on during the natural ups and downs of any project, but there comes a point when you should be able to go about your work in (somewhat affable) silence because the work speaks for itself.

The Egyptian plover bird does not present the crocodile with a monthly report on the hours it put in to teeth cleaning in order to justify its work. The results are seen and felt by the beneficiary in their everyday lives. The plover bird is granted the right to live every time it confidently perches amongst the teeth of a living, breathing crocodile. The crocodile gets an exceptional service from an expert provider. We can all learn something from the lack of bells, whistles, cloaks and daggers in a relationship like that.

So, now that we have identified an excellent working relationship, however obscure, it's time to take a look at the other side of the coin – the shit that really makes life difficult – the toxic client relationship. Rather than take the opportunity to finger point, if we want to be the communications consultants we aspire to, it's our responsibility to ensure there is never be a breakdown in communications.

I have never seen anything more detrimental, yet more common, than the client and advisor bumping heads. Big issue, little issue, non-issue; high or low expectations; there are both clients and consultants who create conflict. You might have even dealt with those who crave and coerce it – the insidious bastards.

Most of the time, there is a naivety and a lack of self-awareness that can absolve most people of maliciously messing things up. They don't even know that they're causing strain. In fact, I guarantee that most of us have done it without even realizing. I know I have. It was possibly the single greatest weakness that I had to address and improve upon as my career progressed. The competitive, winner-takes-all environment I grew up in could no longer frame my view of what success looks like, nor how it is achieved. There became an understandable senselessness in defining every relationship by winners and losers, or givers and takers. For me, it was a huge compromise gap on my part. By simply opening my eyes to the issues caused, it became a gap I was determined to bridge.

Surprisingly, to the competitive spirit I thought I would have to betray to achieve it, the solution was intrinsically linked to discipline. Maybe this was something I could get the hang of. Maybe it was time to think about judo.

Judo is the brainchild of Professor Jigoro Kano, whose life-long dedication to the development of judo and Japanese athletics afforded him the title of "Father of Japanese Sports". After mastering several styles of jujutsu including Kito-Ryu and Tenjin-shinyo Ryu in his youth he began to develop his own system based on modern sports principles.

Dr. Kano, who eventually received a doctorate in judo, undertook a nation-changing role in sport – one which led to his naming as the first Asian representative to the International Olympic Committee in 1909. This was a man with will to interrogate and reframe the established principles of other sports to come to something he thought would be more refined. This was a man we can all learn something from.

The principles of judo are honed by perfecting oneself through "systematic training of the mind and body so that each person works in harmony with themselves, and ultimately with all others". What is most interesting to me, in a world more known for the blood-shedding, money-boasting principles of MMA and professional boxing, is coming to learn that judo is as much about restraint as it is about exertion. In fact, leading judo sensei agree that in any exchange, the judo response is to give way, to not meet force head-on. Let's unpack that.

Discipline, in the judo sense, fundamentally refers to each person's ability to read the other and to act or react appropriately. Am I exposing a weakness of theirs? Am I exploiting a strength of mine? Understanding this, take yourself from the judo mat and picture yourself in a meeting.

You have a notepad on the glass table in front of you, you're surrounded by a minefield of empty coffee cups, and you have those two questions scribbled at the top of a lined notepad page – am I exposing a weakness of someone else, or am I exploiting a strength that I have. When the script is flipped, how does that change your approach to the meeting? Because in the case of a meeting, you actually have a common goal with a single, shared fulcrum – the project, the campaign, the relationship itself. You represent a team, whether it feels like it or not. Am I exposing a weakness of theirs? Ok, then nobody benefits from that. Nothing is achieved by standing on the shoulders of others, not least when those shoulders pay your bills. If you frame every thought, every response and every action in a team meeting with the essential principle that it is best not to expose weaknesses of others, how much less would you say? For me, it was honestly a lot. And remains so. It is a huge turning point in my client relationships and with that, my career. The separation of your strengths and others' weaknesses can be a critical game-changer in your approach to client management. The only step that remained then, from my perspective, was being able to apply these principles to necessary levels of scale.

Most consultants will be hired as a function of a single department or executive office – politician, CEO, department head. The relationship holder on the client side, then, is often called the 'principal'. Just as the term is used in real estate, this is the person that has hired you to act on their behalf, direction or needs. And as we've learned from marriage, crocodiles and judo, this relationship can be a real clusterfuck to get your head around. Well, just wait until we add in their wider circle of influence and you might just face a group of people with lots of say, none of the expertise and no direct relationship with you. Kind of like the fitness influencer industry. Fun times all round.

Sir Alec Issigonis, automotive engineering genius and godfather of the timelessly iconic Mini cars, is credited with one of my favourite quotes of all time:

"A camel is a horse designed by committee."

I never knew an idiom so perfect for work as a consultant in the Middle East. Besides the obvious (80% desert landscape and the importance of camels to the nomadic Bedouin people), the sheer scale and complexity of projects feeds a working environment marred by duplication, complication and obfuscation within the consultancy and client services. I have lost count of the projects that have been derailed and entirely undone by either a failure to agree, or an endless string of compromises. I have even contributed to such failures. When right and wrong are less important than give and take, it requires a special level of awareness to understand that controlled compromise is a tool in our world of professional intangibles.

An engineer can firmly say that a 2cm compromise will cause a 100ft bridge to collapse, but no communications expert can tell for sure the effect of a tweet, or press release, or logo, or even a word, for good or bad. This is an area defined by more than fifty shades of grey. This is where we get decision by committee at its worst.

So, if a committee is a function that keeps minutes and loses hours, our job is to at least ensure that those minutes serve our needs. And hey, chances are we get paid by the hour anyway. To achieve that, it's a matter of give and take – Ok, we might just need to do a whole lot more of giving, but that's fine too. When it comes to our clients – those we may forget lead incredibly complex lives in often-siloed departments within unimaginably complex corporate confines – we need to be the BFF jumping to post heart-eye emojis on their new profile picture, publicly endorsing and propping-up what they say, and privately help and correct where possible. Sound familiar? It should, this is the entire premise of public relations and reputation management.

You see, what we do is diverse and complicated, but who we are is simple – relationship managers. Communications advisory gets a whole lot easier when you find yourself viewing it all on the same terms, from the same role – of the people, for the people. Like we established in the opening chapters, we have a simple role to play in the lives of those who hire us. Externally: support the good, navigate the bad. Privately and internally: quietly work behind the scenes to help everyone stay on the path to success.

The difference between success and failure, I believe, is to take responsibility for the quality and strength of professional relationships by understanding the role of communication in great relationships, and the role of great communicators in facilitating them. So, whether your standard is a happy marriage, a daring bird, or the founder of Judo, the importance of relationships to the success of our work is inescapable. What we do from there is anyone's guess.

CHAPTER SIX

MEET JACK, OF ALL TRADES

"An expert is one who knows more and more about less and less

until he knows absolutely everything about nothing."

- Nicholas Butler

Nobody ever said that the 'Jack of all trades' was a shoddy workman. Who would have thought that needs reminding? The phrase now scoffed at and scorned by an increasingly specialist, professional elite, is actually intended as a compliment. It means versatility, adaptability and above all else, usefulness. When did usefulness stop being so useful? In this chapter, we put the proverbial foot down. It's time to call out the chorus of gobshites and gurus that claim to have the expert solution for every problem; to understand why my Nana stole that Nicholas Butler quote; and to see what we can all learn from the Swiss when it comes to finding function in the most complex forms. Understandably, it all starts with our view of the world of work.

For someone in their mid-twenties, the workforce has a different psyche than anything we had been described before. There is a step-change, from jobs for life and the accessibility of a middle class living, to the digitised, dog-eat-dog world we find ourselves in today – many of the old can't afford to retire, the young are starting even younger, and 30% of people in between now change jobs every 12 months – all seeking more, better, different; and most never finding it. You see, there's a restlessness that permeates the job ladder of the 21st Century, and while it's not an inherently bad thing it sure as shit is tense. Interestingly, the survival instinct seems to lean towards specialism and self-promotion – but I'm not convinced.

I mean, I understand where it starts.

Modern professionals crave some semblance of unique professional purpose. There's no shame in that – even if it sounds egotistical. The endless workdays, inseparability of emails from WhatsApps, lack of weekends, and an unrelenting demand for constant creativity would drive anyone to question if they are any more than an over-qualified butler service. And yet, for all those suffering an understandable existential crisis, this culture of professional pressure has also given rise to the growth a curious group of self-defined, self-professed visionaries – the go-getting gurus. These part-insidious, part-oblivious, human-lymphocytes are the first thing for us to address because they have the ability to turn capable, interesting individuals into the entrepreneur-idolizing, quick-fix-fawning messes that we see around us. "How?" – you might ask, in a world of increasing-educated, information-interrogating professionals? Well, it's actually something called the spiral of silence.

The spiral of silence is a political science and mass communications theory by German theorist, Elisabeth Noelle-Neumann. And, apart from being incredibly important for anyone in the communication professions, it explains a lot about media platforms of self-perpetuated shit-housery like LinkedIn – my gargantuan gripe, as you will come to see.

In brief, Noelle-Neumann observed the innate human fear of isolation as a result of holding seemingly dissenting or minority views, and the effect this shame and fear has on our understanding of public opinion. As we all might recognize from our own lives, when those who think that they hold a minority viewpoint keep these views to themselves for fear of being stigmatised, all we're left with is the increasingly unchecked dominating view of someone who appears to speak for everyone else. What's worse, is people then endorse this view for fear of being left out. Crazy, right?

Well because of it, we (the communications intelligentsia) are left eye-rolling and anger-unfollowing in the nonsense that follows – you know, a post about how "Van Gogh wasn't appreciated until his 30s so that's why I'm taking a gap year to work in an elephant sanctuary in Bali" – and it's exactly what we deserve. On our watch, the would-be corporate engagement tool of LinkedIn has descended into an incredible case study of the spiral of silence in practice – only the outcome of this one fills the online world with endless, generic, pseudo-positivity. For as long as we use the platform to communicate our unrealistic, ultra-professional personas, our attention-seeking brains will be forced to flicker from generic visuals about Sisyphus to the never-did-anything-in-his-life-useless-bastard-connection who liked it. But, as stomach turning as that sounds, you all know that LinkedIn is home to far worse than out-of-context philosophical musings by people you've never met. Now, we must come to a contribution to the world as useful as the 'G' in 'Lasagne', and as genuine as Donal Trump's tan – now, we have the job titles...

- Thinkfluencer

- Chief Thought Provoker

- Chief Listening Officer

- Chief Ideation Officer

- Chief Enlightenment Officer

- Change Facilitator

- PR Guru

- Digital Diva

- Brand Warrior

- SME Superhero

The list, I regret to inform you, grows by the minute. In fact, if I don't have six out of ten connections who exist to "Help companies to find simple solutions to complex challenges", I might just lie awake at night worried about all the companies destined to drown in their own complexities. So, whether you've been victim or perpetrator in this weird game of faux show-and-tell, it's time we all agree to stop the spiral of silence.

Funnily enough, it was my Nana, Eileen Woods, who has long had this all figured out. It was her that I first heard the Nicholas Butler quote from.

"An expert is one who knows more and more about less and less until he knows absolutely everything about nothing", she said.

She worked for more than 65 years of her life, only ever slept a handful of hours a night, and I don't ever remember hearing about her taking a holiday. Having left her native Killorglin, Co. Kerry, to go to England to train as a nurse at the age of 16, to returning and marrying my granddad, Thomas 'Barney' Woods, my Nana worked six or seven days a week as a head postmistress, shopkeeper, switchboard operator, and petrol pump attendant in the same house in Milltown, for the next 60-odd years.

Like the pub and bakery businesses run by the Larkin family across the road, they did what they had to, and what was needed, so that a rural town can survive. Then, as the years went on; as sprawling towns and cities developed across the county, local businesses shut and failed, and the faces and names of those she greeted every day became more and more unfamiliar; she (in her mind) had a continued duty to run the postal service for all who need it. For post users, for social welfare recipients, for the staff she employed. More than that, it's fair to say, she had a reason to get out of bed in the morning.

Despite crippling hip and back issues and an increasingly dangerous job as an elderly, rural postmistress, it honestly took over five years to convince her to retire. That, a full-time job too! But, aside from unrelenting will and a great many other things, what I learned from my Nana Eileen is that purpose, diligence, and a willingness to adapt to changing demands, are far more important than titles, status, and specialism in any workplace.

Usefulness, as and when it is required of you, and as a task demands of you, is tantamount to achieving anything. No matter what day and age you find yourself in. It diminishes the hierarchy, circumvents the title, and asks 'what do you do?'. When I was promoted to be the youngest Associate Director in my company at the time – something I was very proud of – she had the wit to reply, *"That's excellent. And who, or what, do you direct?"*

Good fucking question, I thought. And I'm still trying to figure that one out.

Believe me, I get it – increasing connectivity and competitiveness within our everyday lives has led the professional world to burst at the seams with new job descriptions, roles and functions every year. Often, in ways that do little other than contribute to dilution, rather than specialism. In communications alone, this rate of complex change is increasingly impossible to track. Not only do you have the indescribable pleasure of your immediate family not having a fucking notion what you do every day, you can now turn up at conferences and events within your own sector and meet people with job descriptions you have never heard.

While this may be new and overwhelming for you, as it is for me, it's important to remember that these are the constant aches of growth pains. For example, if we jump back just ten years and the entire social media department of any organisation would not have existed. Traditional media was just *media*. Twitter was only created by Jack Dorsey, Biz Stone, Evan Williams and Noah Glass in March 2006. Facebook advertising was launched at a Mark Zuckerberg hosted event to 250 of the top advertising and marketing executives at a New York event in November 2007. Snapchat, launched in late 2012, feels like it could have been and gone by the time you read this.

A global 2018 survey of the digital marketing industry found that digital advertising spend has risen from 31.8% in 2016, to

38.8% of advertising budgets in 2018. For comparison, the traditional forms of newspaper and outdoor advertising sit at 8.1% and 6.2% respectively. For all the one-channel specialists, traditionalists, and beneficiaries of by-gone times, this means more than a failure to recognise change in audience consumption trends. It quite literally means redundancy. The feeling that you have very little purpose and ever-diminishing value to offer. Whether you're on the wrong end of that realisation or just want to make sure you never find yourself there, the road to redemption is clear: identify, adapt, undertake.

You now have to be useful, flexible, informed, intelligent, tireless, connected, eager, experienced, pliable, adaptable and committed. The best example I've come to describe the type of people we need to be is the Swiss army knife. Of course, as a snowflake millennial, I refer to a Swiss Army Knife in terms of being a great metaphor – I haven't a fucking clue how it gets on in the trenches. So, if I can drag myself away from my smashed avocado existence, it is interesting to examine the concept of multi-tool mentality. What we can learn from that approach, is even more interesting still.

It was in Ibach, Switzerland, in 1884, where Karl Elsener and his mother, Victoria, opened a cutlery cooperative that would soon produce the famous army knives sold to the Swiss Army. The original model, produced after a contract for the Swiss Army Modell 1890 was won that very year, was simply referred to as the Soldier Knife. It was multi-function by design, with the express need to assist soldiers in rifle maintenance and access to their canned food. While the less imaginative of us might have come up with a double-ended device consisting of a screwdriver head on one end and a spoon on the other – a spoondriver? A screwn? – the Elsener model managed to think outside the box, while literally delivering inside the 10cm carved wooden cylinder. After some early feedback and additions, the Soldier Knife included a blade, a reamer, a can opener, a screwdriver, and oak handles.

It was multi-functional because there are many seemingly simple, yet often insurmountable obstacles a soldier may face – sound familiar? Essentially, it is most useful to have many uses. With one of two highly honed skills, you may not be as useless as a paper umbrella, but it's still no good being a bottle opener unless everything you encounter is a bottle top.

The Swiss, in fact, have an unrivalled history of complicated mechanical product design. This is a central pillar of why they always have been, and seem to endlessly remain, the best watch manufacturers in the world. For those who have no interest in horology (the study of the measurement of time), bear with me on this one. Not only is it the, ahem, *timeless* metaphor for functional craft, but it's actually a useful conversation point when those you advise have a wrist adorned with something that costs about five-times your salary.

If you're not familiar with the automatic watch, here's a quick introduction. An automatic or self-winding watch is a mechanical watch in which the natural motion of the wearer provides energy to run the watch, making manual winding unnecessary. On the engineering side of things, automatic watches are made up of anywhere from 100 to 300 individual parts. The terms used to describe both the mechanical engineering parts, and the simplification of aesthetic features, are equally fantastic for those whose job is to simplify the complex for wider audiences. Let's look at one perfect example to start – complications.

Every mechanical watch feature that is added beyond the typical three-hand working (hour, minute and second hand) is endearingly referred to as a complication. Which it certainly is, if you're the person responsible for hand-crafting an extra 100 comparably hair-width metal pieces as a result. However, what is a complication to the watchmaker and the horologists, is a function to the user. This is important – each complication has a function, because it's only worth putting in all those hours of work for something that will be valuable for the user. For watches, these complications include calendars, sub-second timers, annual calendars, moonphases and minute-repeaters. First introduced in the 1930s, highly complicated watches never existed as over-engineered hallmarks of leading international watchmakers, but each came to meet the demands of increasingly multifaceted users.

At the extreme end, the Vacheron Constantin watch that boasts the most parts of any ever created, has 57 complications, a whopping 2,800 individual, hand-made and hand-polished parts, all cased in just a 50.55mm diameter housing. But most automatic complications speak to the functional essence of 'tool-watches' – to be a tool. In dive watches, commonly recognised in the Rolex Submariner, the rotating bezel (outer case of the dial) was designed to track dive times; while pilot watches like those made famous by Breitling or Zenith, are notable for large and easy-to-read Arabic numerals, while others offer reference points for highly sophisticated aviation tools.

The Swiss, in their long-standing mechanical design psyche, understand and embody that a singular focus on task is likely to leave you overtaken by advancements in technology, or menial change in human behaviour. By ensuring the fundamentals are world-class (the most accurate time keeping devices on the planet), while adapting and reinventing to changing needs and behaviours (watches for flights, diving, motor racing, world-travel), the leading Swiss watch makers have created a marque that stands for endlessly useful, multipurpose functionality, at the highest quality of product delivery. If you wake up every morning wondering what you want to be in life, you may not have to look any further than your wrist for the inspiration you need.

So, what is it that we can learn from the approaches of times gone by and people not yet forgotten? Well, it all seems pretty clear – there's a sweet spot to find for us all. Somewhere between an expert and an adapter. The only way to do this is to take a broad-stroke approach to learning. As it was described to me once – to learn to learn, and then learn to love learning. In acknowledging the fundamental value of multi-functionality, we all have to begin to consider a 'have and not need, rather than need and not have' approach. For communications, that means to have brand experience or digital skillsets or design capability, whether you get to use it daily, weekly, monthly or once in a blue moon. So, when it comes to the point in your career when you want to be the shot caller, you find your perfect place, and you want to deliver on every level, just make sure that your menu of options is only limited by your ability to articulate all these skills on a two-page CV.

CHAPTER SEVEN

GO PLAY OUTSIDE

"You have to be in a state of play to design."

- Paula Scher

You can tell by now that I love a play on words. So, as much as I endorse a healthy lifestyle of fresh air, exposure to the elements and a break from the concrete confines of professional life, this chapter is about a different kind of 'outside' – outside the box.

While it takes many forms and encapsulates a great many things, what we're talking about here is creativity. Not only the ability to think differently, but the diligence to arm yourself with the skills and tools to bring those ideas to life in a way that makes the hairs on the back of a neck stand up and clap. This one goes out to the doodlers and PowerPoint perfectionists alike. This one is about the designers. So, if you're not a designer, what's it got to do with you? Well, it depends... how good do you want to be?

****

As the saying goes, variety is the spice of life. If that's true, the communications industry, is spicier than an unexpected habanero in the messy guacamole of our existence. Not only do many of us have the option to try different things throughout our careers, but it's increasingly forced on us to adapt and change just to keep up with our work on a near-annual basis. If we learn how to approach and handle this change, we might be able to get ahead of the curve in our own personal and professional growth paths. From need and not have, to have and not need – as standard operating practice.

Today, most good multi-discipline or integrated communications consultancies do a great job of offering all staff an opportunity to operate within an incredibly varied

121

communications mix. Through fortune, opportunity, will, and sheer curiosity, I've been exposed to a list of disciplines as long as… well, the next few lines, at least. It began with a naïve foray into something called public relations, and at one time or another touched public affairs, management consultancy, project management, sales, professional development, advertising, marketing, branding, social media management, copywriting, speech writing, event management, internal communications, sports marketing, influencer marketing, sponsorship procurement, photography, and design. In many ways, this is why I've expressly referred to "communications" throughout this book – I just don't see the value in drawing hard lines between functions when there's so much crossover to be enjoyed. And yet, with all I've listed and all you may have experienced in your own career, photography and design might be the ones to raise some eyebrows.

To be clear, this chapter is not a call to arm yourself with a DSLR camera and Adobe Design software tomorrow morning. All I'm saying is that you might be pleasantly surprised at how accessible and useful these tools can be for any communications professional of any discipline out there – despite posturing as the preserve of perma-vaping, stubble-sporting, spectacle-wearing specialists.

So, I'll be the first to admit that my love for design is innate. Whether I'm in a café, waiting room, or meeting room, or come across a newsstand or newsfeed, my eyes are always drawn to the contrasts and colours of photography, typography and graphic design. My brain pours over the compositions. My mind whirrs through internal archives to dig out the references that allow this visual, word-free image to communication an idea or feeling. For me, it's the most impressive form of communication because it appears to be the most difficult to do well. In reality, it's not.

Design, once understood, is not rocket science, and it's definitely not otherworldly. Our world, digital and physical, is an endless exhibit for anyone who can take notice of the role of design in our everyday lives. Ask any architect or interior designer and they'll tell you that every space we enter has been created and curated with our feelings in mind; incredible photographers and designers can be found instantly at our fingertips; our eyes can spend their time incessantly flickering from graffiti tags and murals to every shop-front type-face and logo we pass; and anyone can seek out and spend time in art galleries big or small, wherever you are in the world. We're all curating content worthy of a creative or art director's inspiration wall, most of us just haven't realised it yet.

In fact, the effect of this curation on human minds little to do with art, and more to do with science. For a quick but helpful introduction – the way our brains adapt to stimulus is called neuroplasticity. Although it may sound like some sort of weird cosmetic surgery for our brains, it actually refers to the flexibility of the brain as it is shaped and reshaped to respond to new stimuli, experiences, emotions and thought patterns. On the negative side, this pattern-forming mind-mapping exacerbates the persistent, negative thought associated with anxiety, depression and other mental illnesses – something we all need to be aware of when we examine the content we consume. But, the upside of this mental malleability means that positive stimulus can be a deliberate, immediate and life-changing alteration of how we think about things, or how we think about thinking. So, if you think you're not creative enough to understand design, think again.

Without it, there's this established, boundary-breaking function that is often forgotten or disregarded by those of us involved in the wider spectrum of communications planning. We obsess about audiences, platforms, placement and reach, but many of us can't lay out an idea in an engaging way on a PowerPoint slide. Not unlike the Irish border at Brexit, it's important to remember that our impact as communications professionals isn't protected by a vague fall-back plan – the "I'm not a designer" clause. Fuck that. I fully believe that to branch out any strand of our professional skillset, whether copywriting, design or media relations, all we have to do is pay attention to this world that is shaped by content consumption. And if you're as distracted as the rest of us are, one easy way to try force focus on the effect of graphic art and design is to visit a modern art museum. The outcome might just surprise you.

While working from Paris for one week on an international cultural project, I spent six hours one day at Centre Georges Pompidou, home to Musée National d'Art Moderne. I could feel the synaptic sparks fly from the minute I set my eyes on it, and what I came across inside drew me in or pushed me away with an immediacy that's hard to replicate with any other medium. I wandered and worked, blissfully – for the first time in a very long time. Conference call to exhibition; press release to Picasso; it was one of the most creatively inspiring environments you could find yourself doing the work you've always done, on a random Tuesday afternoon in March. My mind came alive. In fact, it did so before I even got inside the door.

In the vein of outside of the box, we have to first talk about the building itself. The architectural experts can argue over the design terminology to define Centre Georges Pompidou - postmodern, constructivist, high-tech, or brutalist - but to the man on the street, the building is simply "inside out". It looks like some grotesquely concocted PR pop-up for a scaffolding company, or a weather-testing space for Crown Paints.

Renzo Piano and Richard Rogers designed the iconic Centre Georges Pompidou building in the 1970s. Piano and Rogers, to their credit, decided to take on more than an architectural brief, and instead took on an entire Parisian view of what art should look like. Their design, with the electrical, technical, sanitary and load-bearing infrastructure entirely outside of the inner artistic space, and the bold external piping of red, green, blue and yellow, closer resembles a playground than what many could imagine for post-modern Paris. That was the point. There's an incredible integrity to what the building is, physically, and what it represents, symbolically. Modern art, by very definition, is art in which the traditions of the past have been thrown aside in a spirit of experimentation. I don't know about you, but I can't think of a better way to house, display and celebrate the greatest collection of modern art in the world, than in a building unapologetically designed to that mission. That is doing your thinking outside the box, and then painting the outside bits in primary colours. Now for what's inside.

The thought of an art gallery can be a scary thing for anyone who hasn't a degree in art history, or those who aren't sure of the difference between a Dali and a Basquiat. So, allow me to let you in on a little secret. In all the art galleries I've been to, all the images I've found myself lost in, and all the designers I have been enamoured by, I've never really read their description for the piece of art. Not one I can recall anyway. And while that may seem ignorant or arrogant or a combination of the two, there's something special to take from it if you work in communications. Art photographer John Paul Caponigro is quoted as saying, "less information leads to more interpretation", and this sweet spot of nuance and context is where neuroplasticity really comes alive – something that can only be a good thing for creators and consumers alike. In our world, what we can take from this is that the more impactful we want our brand communications to be, the less words we should use. The more we should use our communications to show, rather than just to tell. The more we should remember, that not everyone is going to just "get it", because we've spent days or weeks or months creating it. Don't believe me? Well, how about we take a look at some world-famous art that said nothing to me at all.

Jackson Pollock is one of the most critically acclaimed American artists of all time, famed with creating a new form of painting, called abstract expressionism. His art is instantly recognisable by the canvasses splattered, sprayed and splashed with paint in a manner that closer resembles a psychotic episode. To me, on the other hand, Pollock's genre-defining highlights could be

129

matched by any toddler with enough paint and sugary-treats to distract them from the iPad for an hour.

Honestly, that's how ignorant I can be about art. What I'll never be ignorant about, however, is the effect that art can have on people. Impact in the art world may lead to critical success; but understanding how to elicit such impact from communications campaigns is our career game-changer. I can stand in front of the exquisite brushwork of Pablo Picasso or the (eh...) paintings of George W. Bush, and it really doesn't matter what they are trying to capture, convey and communicate. The minute we put our work to the world, we immediately lose control of how it will be received. The audience is "the captain now". So too is everyone we ever hope to communicate with for our work. There's an audience-centricity to art that those of us in boardrooms and open-plan offices can only learn from, yet many within our industries have never cared to look. The artist, through any medium or expression, may tell us what they are saying. If I'm the audience, on the other hand, I decide what it *tells me*.

In a chapter about mavericks and the mastery of mental gymnastics, what we're really trying to do is highlight those rare people who have the ability summon an unconscious feeling within others – no matter what their medium of delivery. More than that though, we have the opportunity to discover what we might learn from them too. Especially when we remember our need to identify, understand, and target the influencers and the influenced, the leaders and the followers, and the lurkers and the latecomers in any audience matrix. What great communicators do exceptionally well is understand the differences and commonality between people at varying levels of scale. And the best learned from artists, designers, architects and innovators to bring that to life in a creative, outside of the box way.

One individual that I have always admired, maybe above all others, is acclaimed shoe designer, Nike design godfather, and all-round cool-fucking-dude, Tinker Hatfield. His ability to move people, literally and emotionally, through design, is unlike anything most of us could ever imagine. Hatfield made his name for the ground-breaking 'air bubble' Nike Air Max midsole, first released in 1987. A shoe, whose inspiration actually came from the Centre Georges Pompidou. As an architectural graduate, his fascination for such an approach to building married with his obsession with sports performance footwear and birthed the most iconic silhouette in the history of sneaker culture – at a time, we would later find, that charged the course of then-struggling Nike. Hatfield, and his predecessor and mentor Bill Bauermann, had been playing with the idea of harnessing air bubble technology to enhance sole responsiveness, comfort and cushioning for athletes for some time. But the inside-out aesthetic of the visual midsole bubble is rightfully attributed to the curiosity, adventurousness and playfulness of Hatfield alone. Hatfield is a master of multi-discipline thinking, because he committed himself to a variety of interests, inspirations and work. The result is something that no shoe designer or architect alone could accomplish.

The final, most powerful element of creative design that I've come to appreciate, is reference and cross-reference. The nod and the wink, or the pick and mix. The Nike Air Max shoe, literally designed for more comfortable walking, involves a brand name taken from the Greek goddess of victory, design technology informed by engineers and scientists, and footwear 'architecture' inspired by a French modern art museum. Eloquently described in documentary by the man himself, "As I often say, when you sit down to design something – it can be anything; a car, a toaster, a house, a tall building, or a shoe – what you draw or what you design is really a culmination of everything you have seen and done in your life, previous to that point".

So, where does it fit into our everyday lives as consultants? Well, if you have ever faced the fiery gauntlet of turning a 500-row excel document of data into a visually represented, brand-aligned, market appropriate, digitally native, CEO-satisfying Infographic formatted for multi-platform dissemination, then you will know the invaluable assurance that comes with a design genius on your team.

For me, the greatest designer I had the pleasure to work with was Brian Wilson of Wilson Creative, in Cork, Ireland. I learned how to learn about design from working with him, and I haven't looked back since.

Brian has a character that effortlessly combines the endless curiosity of a five-year-old, the immediate affability of a life-long friend. Add to that a rate of delivery that would put any logistics service to shame and you have someone that could instil a love for design in the blind. German author, Kurt Wilhelm Marek, under his now infamous pseudonym C.W Ceram wrote, "Genius is the ability to make the complex simple". Brian Wilson is in this most humble, unassuming sense, a communications genius. What I learned from working with him was immeasurable, and what we can all learn from working closely with designers is even greater still.

You see, the main downside with great design, and the great designers, is that they make it all look so easy – something we have a critical role in helping our clients to understand. Great design is never just "Pretty pictures, words on a page" – something I've heard said to a blank-faced, overwhelmed, underpaid, misunderstood millennial intern, as some sort of rousing endorsement to meet a client design brief, from a CEO who assumed 'this is what kids do on their phones all day anyway'. Designers, in so many ways and memes, typify the eternal challenge communications professionals face: everyone will always think they can do your job easily, because everybody communicates. Professionals today (mostly of the male variety) are seemingly biologically engineered to over-assume our own prowess. That looks easy; therefore, it is... It isn't. And so, the eternal battle between understood, appreciated and underestimated continues.

The designers, for their part, keep getting better – as do the tools to surround and support them. What that means for the hyper-connected, digital savvy, communications consultant multi-tool (hopefully, you), is increased, and simplified, access to the skills required. Be that the people equipped to deliver exceptionally creative solutions to our communications challenges, or the software that makes many design-related tasks idiot proof.

I used a free, online design tool to create the cover to this book from scratch, along with any and all marketing materials you may have seen with it. It was conceptualised on a red-eye flight as I was surrounded by hundreds of men in suits, intended to be a nod and a wink to silhouettes of TV show Mad Men, designed over a couple of hours, tested and refined over time, and all pulled together using existing free templates and an acquired understanding of design layout. That's pretty much the example that proves the point I'm trying to make here. You don't have to "appreciate art" in the bespectacled gazing, designer-stubble chin-stroking way you might have been opposed to. You don't have to bore colleagues and friends to death with your story of how Banksy hides his identity because of the role of his anonymity plays as both central to, and inherently separate from, the satirical portrayal of mankind's suffering in his work… But you do have to understand, appreciate and utilise the role, potential and impact of design led, or visually framed communications.

Like everything that we do, there is a utopian ecosystem where every type of communications function, form and facet have a role to play. The creative, the playful, the challenging, the absurd, the simple – the ever engaging and reaction invoking work of designers and design-minded communicators is the dimly lit, inviting room that sets the tone for the enticing words to follow. The importance we place on that has the potential to change the success of our work forever. If not, well, then I hope

you have fun in your little box.

CHAPTER EIGHT

HONESTY AS POLICY

"If it is not right do not do it; if it is not true do not say it."

\- Marcus Aurelius

The pervasive rise of image-altering and the dilution of fact to 'fake news' has brought about more trust issues than a 20-something who caught a glance at their other half's DMs. You see, all it not as it seems. Not least when we fail to take our eyes off the screens. Grandstanding statements by headline grabbing commentators, online echo chambers left unchecked, and the outright outrage regularly expressed on social media is only serving to compound a culture of hysteria that would put the Cold War to shame.

Shouts defiantly – We, the people, no longer trust the institutions of society!

With good reason, too. From Facebook to Volkswagen to whichever man-bastard last cheated on a Kardashian, we have had to deal with a lot of shit from brands we have invested in – emotionally, financially, or otherwise. As the bridges burn, we demand more than ever. At minimum, unshakeable honesty, integrity and transparency from almost anyone in the public eye today – and that applies to anyone who takes a second of our time, or a cent of our money. Understandable, of course. But fair? Maybe not.

When the masses demand that their heroes, sports stars, politicians, CEOs, celebrities, and telecom provider's customer service agents be instantly, voyeuristically accessible at any time of the day (or night), the masses invariably crumble when this leads them to see a side of their demi-god that is a little harder to swallow. Not least when those who are accessible have to be infallible and human, stoic and passionate, analytical and personable, and driven and tempered, all at the same time. We're a fickle, whiney bunch when we want to be, and the fallout can be immediate – volatile market swings, rapid and vapid leaderships changes, court cases, restraining orders, redundancies, bankruptcy, death. Needless to say, all sides are a bit fucking stressed as a result.

Whispers apprehensively - We, the communications industry, have a responsibility to understand, rebuild and re-establish the acts that ensure trust-building between our clients and their most important audiences.

'Acts', you'll see, is the crux of all of this.

Practically speaking, trust-building is a very straightforward thing to explain: the closely intertwined relationship between what we say and what we do. No surprise that the ancient Greeks had this figured out years ago. As opposed to a more modern obsession with Insta-affirmation and literal 'likability', trust between people has always depended upon a predictability factor. You know, when expectation meets reality – for better or for worse. And while it might be easier to blame a culture of deceit on one side, and a default of crippling mistrust on the other, there aren't enough people starting with the part they can control: themselves.

In a pair of examples you couldn't find together anywhere else on this earth (I checked), I'll unpack the damaging effect of misleading others for personal gain, and the fallibility of pretending to be something that you are not, as a harsh reminder about how easy it is to lose sight of the big picture to achieve a so-called quick win.

With that admittedly obscure introduction, let me tell you why the Taoiseach (Irish Prime Minister) has fleet-footedly strayed from the path of the righteous, along with why you should never believe a capuchin monkey.

****

You've probably come across white-faced capuchin monkeys before. Not only are they the furry friend of many of your favourite nineties TV characters (Ross Geller's pet monkey, Marcel) but they also feature on almost every nature documentary you have seen.

I love nature documents, especially ones about animals. Wildlife documentaries are like a window to the soul for anyone with an abstract mind and a fascination by how the world works. Their ability to dissect, analyse and 'humanize' the way any species interacts can provide a whole new world of learning for us communications experts. I also strongly believe that if ultra-HD micro-camera technology will allow me to see if a mosquito's eyes close when it sneezes, you best believe that I want to know how those blood-sucking little bastards do it. Capuchins, for their part, sneeze like we do. More importantly, they are a great case study in group communications, honesty and distrust.

Primate society, without screens or digital networks to divide it, relies on sophisticated levels of what we would recognize as emotional intelligence. Research carried out by primatologists across the various species has shown that many types of monkeys feel very strongly about fairness. More interesting still is that primates care about perceived fairness to others, by others, in a manner not unlike millennials do. What this means for trust and reciprocity within troops of primates is near mirror-image to the world as we might know it.

So, in order to avoid the tired case studies about Enron and the Clinton-Lewinsky affair, let's take the example of the negative effect of a lie on a troop of capuchin monkeys to show that when a lie is ventured, nothing is gained.

In amazing similarity to human language, biologists have noted that these monkeys have very specific calls which specifically relate to a wide variety of predators – snakes, jaguars, hawks, and eagles, for example, offer daily reasons to scream and shout. In practice, the system is built on the shared values of the troop's survival and is strictly adhered to at all times. Well, almost all times.

Monkey business, as the name suggests, is not run on the principles of socialism. Like many of their primate counterparts, capuchin monkeys live within a very hierarchical society. There are winners and there are losers; the 'haves' and 'have nots' of the troop. Fairness is central to the social contract, as we have established, but the 'stock' of individual capuchin's character can nose-dive with a single misstep.

Picture the scene. You're a social-climbing capuchin in a teaming, scurrying troop of twenty. Well-known, perhaps, but not always well-liked; you begin to wonder if these lice-picking primates could possibly realize how amazing a monkey you truly are. After a day navigating the maze of treetops within your territory, a small cluster of fresh fruit is spotted. The delighted shriek of "Mangos!" rings out within the travelling party. What a time to be alive.

It's actually been a while since your last decent meal. Sure, you can survive off scraps, but it's no way to live. Not for you. You're a special monkey, even if nobody has taken notice. What you have noticed, however, is that this cluster of fruit is a little light on stock, and there definitely isn't going to be enough for anyone to really sink their teeth into.

Hungry and opportunistic, you see your chance.

"Snake!", you cry, with a voracity that shocks most others in to action long before their conscious minds have time to catch up. The troop scatters, passing on the call as they leap, immediately dropping their food, and running for cover. This is not time to fight, they think, it's not worth the risk. Fright, flight and live to fight another day.

The fools.

For you on the other hand, the spoils of war. The sweet taste of success. The immediate fuel and nourishment of a long-awaited and much needed break from the struggles of your reality. Or is it?

As the frantic shouting and screeching ends, everyone's alertness soon alerts them to you, happily munching away on more fruit than you could possibly swallow. You've been found out for what you are – a liar – and the social contract has been broken.

What you have failed to realize, like the boy who cried wolf, is that people (or monkeys) don't like when their trust is betrayed, and a shared system of trust that took a lifetime to build has swiftly been destroyed. Lies, no matter how subtle, clever, or dastardly, have a way of coming back to haunt you. Taking this out of the jungle and into the offices, agencies and desks we swing from – metaphorically or otherwise – the long-standing, hard-earned reputation of your own organisation and those of every client should never be put at risk for smart remark or blatant bluff. Despite the temptation, silence is better than a non-truth, and infamy is never worth the short-term influence.

And yet, as we bang the drum to and for those we represent, deep down we also know that the lies we tell ourselves can be even more dangerous.

To the outside world, Leo Varadkar is the embodiment of an Ireland they didn't know existed. Maybe one they didn't think could exist.

He is young, becoming Taoiseach in June 2017 at 38 years of age; he is non-white; born to an Indian, Hindu father, and Irish,

Catholic mother; and openly gay. When Varadkar's partner, Matthew Barrett, accompanied him to a 2019 St. Patrick's Day dinner with the ultra-conservative Christian Vice President of the United States of America, Mike Pence and his wife Karen, the moment was heralded around the world as another part of Ireland's 'coming out' from decades of Roman Catholic control – a natural step, after Ireland became the first country in the world to legalize same-sex marriage by popular vote in 2015.

This was, for all intents and purposes, a new type of leadership for a new type of Ireland. As the Financial Times put it in a glowing 2017 profile, Leo Varadkar was "the bright young man leading the Irish revival".

Those closer to home, however, have consistently struggled with the realities of a global media darling. In an all too common slight on our profession, Varadkar has been slammed as a "PR obsessed" politician: perma-filtered, photo-seeking, silly-sock-wearing. We, however, know that PR is not inherently evil. What commentators and detractors have failed to realize is that the Taoiseach has not been found out as a scheming spinster, but rather reliant on a poor man's version of PR. Let me explain.

Above all else, the often-misunderstood process of reputation management is about credibility. An honest portrayal of what you say and do. Amplify the good, navigate the not so good. As someone who allegedly takes great pride in his media savvy, Varadkar has lost sight of one important element: what it does not mean, is control.

At a time where most in the industry would agree that the "influencer industry" has completely lost the run of itself with face-tuning, ab-altering and colour-saturating to the point of parody, Varadkar has fallen into the political equivalent of 'Living His Best Life'. From cringeworthy pro-government advertorials that would make an autocratic government giggle, to shiny new tech offices, sunny jogs with political leaders through the Phoenix park, and flag-waving pride marches, there is a lack of tact that often makes him unrelatable. Which is a shame.

The distance forged between idealistic and realistic can be a real career killer for elected representatives, as it loses sight of the grounding purpose of the role – representing real people. While the best intentions of being a modern, digitally accessible leader may have guided Varadkar and his team, he wants to be have stumbled senselessly into something that might not exist beyond a phone screen.

Like Icarus, and anyone who has "influencer" in their bio, the risk is believing one's own hype. All of the items listed above are real world examples from the Taoiseach's life, many that would be a breath of fresh air the policy demystifying day to day work of political advisors, but it's when these are all that we are fed that I have to worry about the advice being provided.

Any communications advisor or strategist who recommends exclusively to promote the good, without at least acknowledging the work still to be done, is doing their client a disservice, not least in politics. This is one of the toughest, most physically and mentally compromising industries to operate within. You have to identify 'big picture' policies that guide improvement at scale, while accommodating or sometimes failing individuals or sectors to achieve it. If we look at the core, Varadkar is failing in communications approach, which is only perpetuated in many forms of execution. A hammer can be used to drive a nail, or it can be used to bludgeon someone's head in. The takeaway for us is to know that the problem is not with the tool, but how it's used.

It is as simple and boring as that, no matter how creatively executed.

****

As I've been at pains to stress throughout this book, audiences are now hard-wired for the dopamine hit of immediate gratification. With that, the lure of content that bags ego-feeding statistics offers a tempting mirage of communications success. The question, then, is posed: are you the communicator they want, or the one they need? Dopamine dealer or communications counsellor. The choice is yours.

When the world around us has descended into fake news, non-truths, and porky pies, every brand, organization, corporation and individual has the ability to decide whether the short-term gain is worth the often-irredeemable long-term loss. It's what separates the communications professionals from people with the ability to communicate. It what separates us (I hope) from them.

And if you still need convincing, I can honestly say that I've never met a communications challenge of any scale, in any part of the world, for any type of business, that wasn't overcome by a simple adherence to integrity, nor one that was not entirely undone by a lack of it. The principles that build, or break, trust between friends, colleagues, neighbours or capuchin monkeys, are no different to the principles that apply to the comparatively abstract beneficiaries of our services: brands, organisations, service providers, governments.

What you do will always outmatch what you say, and actions will always speak louder than words.

This is the honesty policy.

CHAPTER NINE

THE FINAL PIECE

"If you cannot measure it, you cannot improve it"

- Lord Kelvin

Picture the scene.

You've just presented your mind-blowing new campaign pitch to resounding positive feedback, eager client follow-up and an equally impressed boss. Through years of ups and downs, there's an overwhelming appreciation that this is a rare high for an exhausting Tuesday afternoon in a coffee-stained conference room. Suddenly, it all takes a turn for the worst. The imaginary, presentation-smashing confetti seemingly turns to ash; swiftly replaced by darting sideways glances, timid shuffling and squirming in our seat, the glow of our ever-reddening cheeks, and the creeping crawl down our spine that leaves the hair on our head standing to attention.

When your client asks, "How does this measure against our KPIs", it triggers a level of discomfort previously reserved for the moment your parents asked to talk about safe sex. No matter how far you have or haven't ventured, there's a sinking acceptance that you definitely don't have your head around it all yet.

For the last few decades, despite several summits, forums and debates, we haven't really moved the dial on, well, our ability to measure how we move the dial – at least not in a consensus achieving, meaningful way. As a result, there's been very little collective concern. Instead, we are left with the number-crunching optimists (there's more data available than ever before!), the fad-questioning realists (the tools are there, we might just be focusing on the wrong things), or a career-questioning nihilists (my life is a lie, I should have been an accountant). If you're anything like me, you can identify with any camp on any given day of the week. But a problem shared is a problem halved, so this chapter should leave us all with a little more understanding of the status quo and issues at play.

For starters, let's examine the overhaul efforts to date.

In 2010, the PR and communications industry saw the launch of a seemingly exotic new approach, the "Barcelona Principles". They were a bold, new, industry-wide standard for measurement of the practice that was designed as a marked step away from the utterly 'makey-uppy' Advertising Value Equivalent (AVE). AVE was established under the principle that a pitched and 'earned' (not directly paid for placement) piece of media coverage is 'more valuable' than a traditional advertisement. The value of this coverage, it was alleged, was an agency-determined multiple of 'how much harder' that particular slot was to earn, as opposed to buy – often ranging from between 2x and 10x advertising cost. So, your 6-by-4-inch column in the left-hand corner of page 27 may have cost $3,000 to place an ad in, but 'earned' $15,000 in coverage for your ever-indebted client.

Madness, I know.

But credit where credit is due, that is why the Barcelona Principles were devised. An international working group led by a number of global PR bodies came together with the sole purpose of making deliberate, much-needed change. The industry knew there was a problem with fudging the numbers and this acknowledgement and attempt to address it should have been huge – but it wasn't.

Unfortunately, as we all know, change is a lot harder to implement than to define. Despite suitable industry aplomb, and a bit of bluster in monthly newsletter digests, the communications industry continued to grow, diversify, specialise and expand to increasing client demand, while the anoraks, gurus and academics continued to play around with boring old measurement. The reality is that most people working in the industry were too busy, uninvested and disconnected from the conversation to notice it happened at all. And the clients? Well, they were too concerned with their own metrics, budgets and internal KPIs to even know it was happening. You might say it's almost beginning to sound like a communications problem...

So, it was time to try again. 2015 brought Barcelona 2.0. For all intents and purposes, it was another positive move to redefine the impact of work delivered by a bona fide multi-million-dollar global industry. The problem, however, remained the same. Both sets of frameworks were good at identifying the nonsense in current measurement practice, but both were invariably broad, vague and open to interpretation when it came to a clearly defined solution.

The reaction, if you can call it that, was even more muted than before. Few knew what had happened, fewer still cared what it meant; nobody found an impactful, consistent blueprint for betterment. And while it is not for lack of effort, or a reflection of a poor standard of work, the communications industry appears determined to disown the final piece in our otherwise perfect professional picture. Why? I'm not entirely sure.

Undoubtedly, it can be very hard to know where to start. Communications delivery is incredibly intangible at times – there's unavoidable puffery of numbers, the whim of creative subjectivity, the mood of the people we deal with, perceptions changing with the winds, lofty objectives – but what we're trying to achieve isn't intangible. It can't be. We're often just afraid to look. So, rather than a #disruptive solution to measurement, I've found that it's best to examine history (of the professional and ancient varieties), along with some outsider influence, to find a surprisingly applicable direction of travel. Have you ever heard the one about the man who measured the earth before anyone had mapped it? No? Good. But first, let me tell you a little bit about my Dad.

When I was growing up, measurement was a very straightforward affair. It was tactile and tangible. It involved the plastic ruler in a school pencil case, the lines on a football pitch, or whittling down the descending miles on the road signs to visit grandparents in Cork. Maybe I've slipped on my rose-tinted glasses for this chapter, but it feels as though life was a lot simpler back then. It was a world that was measured and, for a time, my prepubescent, perfectionist soul was content.

I used to work with my Dad, Jimmy, over school holidays. He's a carpenter by trade and a woodwork and technical graphics teacher by profession, so that meant long summers filled with the sweet swell of wood shavings. When he needed an extra pair of hands for jobs like decking, hanging doors, or fitting wardrobes, I was more than happy to spend the day working with him. Whether I've told him or not, I have always idolized my Dad's work ethic. While we have to credit our Mam, Áine, for our academic curiosity, it is Dad's critical attention to detail that shaped my view of the world of work for many years to come.

My father is a man who is quietly, restlessly passionate about his craft. He long subscribed to magazines only available on the shelves in America, downloaded detailed video tutorials as he first got to grips with YouTube, and always turned his hand to a left-field request – be that a stilted treehouse with a functioning trap door for us in the back garden, or a quarter-pipe skateboard ramp in the front.

In those days, however, there was no doubting that my role in this environment was a lot more passive. The help I gave my Dad was embodied by the unrelenting contortion of my slender teenage frame: nervously carrying doors and skirting boards up winding stairs, terrified of leaving a scrape on the wall, or begrudgingly pinching the small metal end of the measuring tape against the edge of something as he wandered off to a point across the room. "37 and a half", he'd mutter aloud – entirely for his own benefit. "Six and a half", I'd think in response – the hours left until I get back kicking a ball around!

If you have ever carried a door up four flights of stairs to a converted attic – which includes agonizingly grasping at the fringes with finger strength worthy of one of Yosemite's heroic Dawn Wall climbers, and then held it hovering an inch of the ground to be fixed on the hinges – you learn a lot about your ability to endure hard work. When it's immediately followed by your Dad stepping back with a sigh, "Bollocks, 2 mil' off at the top", you then learn a few very important things about measurement:

1. Do it right or don't do it at all – no matter what the immediate burden.

2. The sum of many small details leads to the perfect result – smooth finishes, flush joints, clean lines. No matter the

role or the industry, the soft touches can have the heaviest impact.

3. And finally, don't ever become a carpenter unless you give a shit about the specific items listed in point two.

My Dad, as I mentioned, is a man of obsessive precision. He carries a measuring tape on the belt, a pencil on the ear, and all sorts of angular rulers in the van. You could say that the integrity of his job is shaped by near-surgical use of materials in a clearly defined space. Floorboards have to cover the absolute amount of floor space, counters have to rest comfortably atop the benches that support them, doors should fit seamlessly within frames. Anything a carpenter might turn his hand to must be delivered with the precision that is most often only noticed when it is lacking. Before all that, the job must be scoped, resourced, timed, and completed – all to meet or exceed the client hopes for their home.

It's strange that after all these years in client services, I only recently drew the comparisons to my chosen profession. It got me thinking... where else could I look for inspiration? Ah, yes – the old reliable, Ancient Greece.

****

Ancient Greek mathematician, Eratosthenes, wasn't afraid to try and measure the seemingly immeasurable. And if you haven't come across him before, you're in for a real nerd-sized nugget of a treat.

Eratosthenes, above all else, was an exceptional intellect. He wrote at length about philosophy, is credited with coining the discipline of geography, contributed immensely to mathematics and astrology, and even penned comedy and poetry. With that, there was only one job suitable of his contribution to society: Director of the Library of Alexandria. Undoubtedly, one of the greatest scholarly roles of his Age.

As Director, Eratosthenes had the ancient-history-equivalent of the only computer in the world – hundreds of thousands of scrolls, cataloguing the most elucidating theories in history, philosophy and a wide range of the ancient sciences. With the greatest wealth of knowledge in living history at his disposal, you would think that anyone would be overwhelmed with the task of taking in all the information at his disposal, never mind worrying about the unknown. Like so many great thinkers, however, Eratosthenes was burdened with the realisation that the more he knew, the more he didn't know. It was this insatiable thirst for understanding that led him to the greatest measurement attempt of his time.

In 240 BC, Eratosthenes measured the circumference of the earth to what modern day mathematicians equate to being within a few per cent of the correct distance – 40,008 kilometres (24,860 miles). The apparent simplicity of the 'how' is even more unbelievable.

As the story goes, Eratosthenes had heard that in Syene, a city south of Alexandria, there were no vertical shadows cast at midday on the summer solstice. Remarkable, he thought. Ever the curious mind, he then wondered if this were also true in his new home, Alexandria. Taking a highly sophisticated measuring device (a stick) and utilizing the research environment at his disposal (the ground; he put a stick in the ground), Eratosthenes found that despite the noon sunlight, a slight shadow was cast on Alexandrian soil. He concluded that if Alexandra had a shadow and Syene didn't at the same time on the same day, the earth's surface was indeed curved. After a few calculations of the shadow length he deemed it to be just over 7 degrees of difference.

Eratosthenes had it. And yet, he couldn't stop there. The calculations went on. Seven degrees of difference equated to 5,000 stadia (the known ancient metric distance between the cities, said to be 800km), 7.2 degrees is 1/50 of 360 degrees, 800 times 50 is 40,000 kilometres.

Mic drop.

The seemingly impossible task of measuring the circumference of the earth, when most of it was yet to be mapped by a single Empire, was achieved by a combination of deductive reasoning, imaginative thinking, and tangible mathematics. More importantly still, the tool that delivered such sophisticated data was a stick in the ground.

So, you might ask, "What has this got to do with me?". Well, quite a lot actually. The Eratosthenes example typifies how we've allowed ourselves to be ignorant of what is possible to measure, in favour of obsessing about all the sophisticated tools and data which can overwhelm with information that is often unnecessary to measure. What we're missing, is someone to stand up and say, "Hey – what's the point of this? What are we trying to achieve?" Because it should be to accomplish something. Something specific.

****

From over exposure to the ill-informed and no meaningful way to enforce industry best practice, communications newcomers are often led down the path of least resistance – the one that suggests that media clippings, retweets, views, shares, likes, or a WhatsApp from your auntie who saw it on "The Facebook", are what success truly looks like. In fairness to the uninitiated, there's a familiarity to those metrics that's very hard to fault. Everyone today is a publisher, content creator and platform user. Why then isn't a successful selfie the same as a successful communications campaign?

As we know, the ability to use a tool and the ability to master it are not one and the same. The goal should not be to get in the paper, or on TV, or on a famous blogger's newsfeed, but to reach and engage the audience on the other side in a way that contribute to wider business objectives. Where good becomes great – a key theme for anyone who picks up this book – is at the moment when the focus turns from measuring outputs to outcomes.

Funnily enough, this is where it all began, and this final example highlights the purposeful, big picture, outcome-focused communications.

If you didn't already know, Edward Bernays (1891 – 1995) is the Father of Public Relations. Those who have come across the life and work of Bernays have failed to decide if he was a publicity revolutionary, a nefarious propagandist or a psychological spinster, but how he began to approach communications challenges is refreshing when compared to the maelstrom of data-driven-drivel served up today.

From his first book, Crystalizing Public Opinion, in 1923, to The Engineering of Consent over 30 years later, Bernays was an innovative, insatiable student of solving business problems. With little or no professional competition, or certainly none that had the chance to develop its own jargon, rules and ideas of success, Bernays was compelled to deal with business and political leaders on their terms, to deliver on their idea of success. The early validity this offered his work is critical, and it only takes one example to see why.

In 1920s America, the luggage companies had an unusual problem for a country with a relatively mobile and inter-connected national population. Americans were travelling more than ever – but buying less and smaller luggage. Why? Well, funnily enough, the products made were so well produced that they rarely, if ever, needed replacing. Those that did, were simply fixed by a local upholsterer. Naturally, this greatly affected the manufacturers margins and significantly diminished the return customer base. As is common of many modern industry lobbies, the luggage manufacturers represented an industry of excess supply and waning demand. The business case for a new approach was laid and Bernays knew that solving this sales problem would be the single metric for which his work will be judged. The singular goal: increase demand (and subsequently sales) of larger luggage bags. The means: amazingly varied.

With a strategy that could hold its own in any leading agency today, Bernays took a holistic, multi-pronged approach to get new baggage into the hands of those the industry most desired. Take a deep breath, it's time to look at the full extent of Edward Bernays in action.

With the singular intention of driving new luggage sales, Bernays sent articles to magazines titled "What the Well-Dressed Woman Wears on a Weekend", stressing the need for women to travel with a varied wardrobe; advised hoteliers to stress in their accommodation descriptions the different sorts of activities their guests would be involved with, and the need for different clothes for each activity; gave luggage to movies and plays to redefine the desirability of the product within the 'story' of travel; created the Luggage Information Service, to be an easy point of call for any journalist or salesperson who wanted to know more about luggage; suggested health officials emphasize the importance that a person should own their own luggage; lobbied foreign embassies to help increase the free weight allowance for those travelling abroad; encouraged stores to put luggage in window displays, and to show the relationship between new clothes styles and new luggage styles; wrote to colleges and universities to send their new intake lists of the clothes and luggage they would need before arriving; urged architects to allot suitable space for luggage storage; wrote to 66 railway companies and 10 steamship companies and urged them to make sure their designers left plenty of room for luggage.

The rest, as they say, is history. The luggage industry boomed for years to come (at least until the Great Depression) and Bernays went on to devise captivating communications campaigns for Lucky Strike cigarettes, Proctor & Gamble, and the 1939 World's Fair in New York, among many others. Edward Bernays succeeded because he delivered tangible, business-building impact as an outcome of strategic, engaging communications. He was research driven, psychology-obsessed, and solely responsible for delivery. Maybe, more to his advantage than has ever been acknowledged before.

Since the unimaginable growth from a one-man innovator to a thriving, multi-faceted industry-level ecosystem, diversity has proven a gift and a curse for the particular task of measurement. It can too often be 'each to their own', as marketing, PR, advertising, social media and internal communications fight for individual praise and, more importantly, individual budgets. Senior communications advisors, be they in-house or consultants, must bear the responsibility of holding the collective consciousness. Because if the communications industry can learn anything from carpenters, ancient Greek mathematicians and the founder or our professional field, it's that the ends are the only determinant of the means, and that success can only be the sum of many well-executed elements.

As the curtain calls, I'll leave you with this final thought from George Bernard Shaw: "The single biggest problem in communication is the illusion that it has taken place". We then, have the unshakeable responsibility for sorting impact from illusion. How exactly we do that remains a conversation worth having.

Come @ me and let's see if we can figure it out together.

CHAPTER TEN

TAILORED THINKING

"Simplicity is the ultimate sophistication"

- *Leonardo Da Vinci*

Here we are – the final chapter.

With (almost) enough said, and much left in the real world to be done, our only remaining task is to refine and reiterate the core principles of communications that supply the meat of this paper-backed sandwich. By bringing it all together in analogical conclusion, we can agree on the imperfect picture of the who, what, why, and how, of our work in communications advisory. As our challenges rise in tandem with our ever-evolving complexity obsession, there's still opportunity to reframe the most important industry-level conversations needed to put our roles back where they belong – on the front-lines and top-tables of organisations, filling our boots with work that actually moves the dials that matter. With that at the fore of our minds, you would think that the next steps are simple – and yet, seeking simplicity remains one of the biggest roadblocks to our progress.

As a word, 'simple' has the misfortune of serving as a one-word crutch for the least engaging communicators among us, triumphantly tacked at the end of the weakest and leakiest statements. "Simple!", they (always 'they') conclude, as you try to wrap your head around the latest ill-informed nonsense to drivel from their overly assertive lips. In reality, it would *simply* be better if they stopped sharing their opinion as fact. These days, you see, the word simple is central to the mansplainers' manifesto, and only positively used to describe aesthetically-soothing Scandinavian design – something, I think, that causes us all to lose out. Although we hardly need more reminding, it's clear by now that complexity is not always king.

One telling example to bring this point to life is in the ever-advancing realm of in-car technology. Buckle up for this one, because it's a constant reminder of just how deadly consumer-demanding complexity can be. The learning for us, too, will become very clear.

To the dismay of safety advocates around the world, car manufacturers began inserting internet-connected computer in motorists' line of sight as early as the mid-2000s. Today, LED screens can be found is the most basic and accessible models across the globe. And the boundary-pushing brands have completely lost the plot with multi-colour displays, in-cabin fluorescent lighting, and eight-directional electronic seat movement – one Italian manufacturer even attempted a centre-console espresso machine!

Helplessly losing their way from useful, understandable resources, like navigation guides, traffic warnings, and weather updates, service providers have again proven our innate inability to reign ourselves in from the realms of possible, to the realities of necessary and beneficial. The pervasive rise of now common-place features such as internet browsing, WiFi connectivity, touch-display, WhatsApp messaging, and even Netflix (on Tesla's 17-inch tablet screen), mean that the industry's alleged bidding to get us to look up from our smartphones has only got us to look as far as the infotainment systems – the road, it seems, is not interesting enough as it is.

When the passenger-focused excuse is dispelled with the fact that 85% of American cars have just one occupant, the driver, what is the real-world benefit of catering to all those twitchy-fingered, dopamine-craving motorists? Well – outside of making money from appeasing market demand – the answer is nothing. And therein lies the problem. You might already see where I'm going with this.

The last three to five years of communications industry 'census' from the UK, US, and the Middle East, for example, all show that Communications is a "profession"-seeking practice. There's an intense, industry-leading desire to be put on par with lawyers, financial advisors and operations officers. With that in mind, there is something that should stick in the craw about service and product providers who bow to every whim of a relatively ill-informed, ADD-displaying consumer base – rather than working with them to define valuable needs that fall within service providers' expertise. In our realm, when there's an uphill battle to establish the value of our own industries, any approach that fails to put professional integrity and responsibility at the core of all innovation in product and practice, is doing us all a disservice. The Chicago Tribune superbly surmised that the motor industry has has fallen prey to "reinventing the wheel for no reason", and you may have seen many product and service offerings in communications that do the same.

As with most of our day-to-day experiences in the oversaturated world of Industry 4.0, we're all suffering at the hands of our insatiable complexity obsession. And, as you well know, communications industries have the benefit of being some of the most transformative and tumultuous around. When notifications whirr, inboxes overflow and the hours melt into an endless malaise, we end up too busy to take ideas, strategies, tactics, plans and even sentences to their most effective and productive form. I don't know about you, but it can feel like weeks on end where I'm too tired to think, too exhausted to explain, too focused to be flexible, too stressed to strength test. The result is a cycle of cynicism that can sap creativity and keeps us looking at outputs (media clippings, retweets, shares) rather than outcomes (increasing purchase desire, brand recall, first preference).

Simplicity, as Da Vinci noted, is the ultimate sophistication. 'Simple' solutions, then, are not simple to come by. And yet, simplicity has the ability to free us from the suffocating shackles of convoluted complexity of our content-obsessed minds. How then, do we achieve it? The problem, in my experience, can only be parsed by forcing ourselves to think differently, to seek new ideas, to court dissenting voices. Whatever you do to get yourself to think about simplicity, there's a world outside our industry that's bursting with much-needed clues.

In a manner befitting of the cover of this book, and the many puns that followed, it should come as no surprise that bespoke tailoring has always fascinated me. Once understood, it's easy to see how this craft offers the ultimate expression of complex craftmanship distilled to seamless simplicity. You may also be surprised to find that it's the perfect closing analogy to our own work as communications consultants.

The artisan craft of bespoke tailoring carries a title that threads from the eloquent Latin origins of "speaking your requirements", to unique needs and lives of individual clients around the globe. If we're honest, many client services don't always serve the client, so it's easy to under-estimate how clearly this interaction-rooted process guides everything the needle touches thereafter.

Let's take a few broad strokes for comparison.

There's the distinct house style for the tailor, honed through the experience and training of individual tailors, and not unlike the differences between a brand, corporate, or digital PR agency; the core tailor-client relationship to be developed, often beginning with an obligatory chemistry-testing coffee-side chat alone, which should sound familiar to anyone who has been to new client meetings; and a collaborative approach, where client preference must be seamlessly integrated with the expertise and recommendations of the experienced tailor, which is a true earmark of any successful campaign of strategy I've had the opportunity to be involved with. As with most client servicing, the sweet spot is a delicate dance of give and take too. A client-dictated suit fails to accommodate the needs of their individual body shape, on one hand. Tailor-dictated suits, on the other hand, can feel like an over-priced spectator sport, lacking the irreplaceable personal touch that you might expect for the relatively expensive cost and time commitment.

A bespoke suit, you see, can take anywhere from three and five fittings, over eight weeks, for anywhere from $1,500 to $8,000 and up. And yet, the cost of the suit doesn't increase with more fittings, more adjustments or more time to complete. Tailors, for better or worse, are ultimately bound by their commitment to the best final product, and it's worth considering how this approach would change our view of the work we spend our lives on. Outcomes, regardless of means, and time-taken, are what the client pays us for. Why, then, do we spend so much time and money billing people for the means?

Bill Gates allegedly said, "If I was down to my last dollar, I'd spend it on public relations" – a quote I will say has never been sourced, verified or confirmed – but he wouldn't have used his last dollar on a billable hour of planning without any action or outcome as a result. Helping a client to achieve the best result, for their needs and means, is a natural next step for our industry – interestingly, harking back to the work of the industry-forming maverick, Edward Bernays. Whether that means more or less work, then, is entirely up to you.

I'm glad to say that there are many practitioners and firms that do this already – some I have even had the pleasure of working with and for – but there's a silent, sheepish majority who continue to provide and charge for hours of services that have little true value for their clients. It's great to know that by learning from other industries, and taking small steps in our approach, the communications industry no longer needs to work that way. And, if I can go full 'TedTalk' without being sued, I'd say "that is an idea worth sharing!"

****

Although I have ruthlessly avoided chapter-summaries and over-egged learnings, allow me to use the remaining words as a final, concise distillation of the takeaways and tales of this book. If nothing else, let it be the easily accessible ammunition to challenge these thoughts and ideas with me on Twitter!

In Chapter One, we exposed a new world order and defined the chaotic consumption habits that lead us to an overwhelming ability to access information at anytime, anywhere, about anything. Communicators and audiences are understandably struggling as a result, and trend-hacking gurus and self-proclaimed game-changers have offered little in the way of valuable respite. Thankfully, by defining the problem, we can now carve the lines between what is worth pursuing, stressing about, and reworking, and all the noise and nonsense that isn't. As big conversations go, it was just the place to start.

Mild-Mannered Mercenaries married crippling existentialism and much-needed light relief. As we all needed to hear, this really is a tricky business. We're the inside-outsiders who are so unsure of our place in the world that an innocent question about our job is more than enough to blow self-esteem to smithereens. But that's OK. Within the consultancy industries, there's an understanding that the core skill is problem solving. We, the communications consultants, just weren't starting in the right place – with ourselves. By parking ego and repackaging expertise, we can succeed where the American and Russian military experts failed, in realising that our level of technical expertise is nothing compared to the ability to successfully impart that knowledge. We are problem-solving communicators; we might just need to communicate our solutions better to start.

Chapter Three: A Fisherman's Tale continued the profound soul-searching, as we attempted to understand the difference between those who communicate, and the skills, tactics and purpose of communications professionals. With widespread content creation, platform proliferation and even emojification in our midst, the path to professional success may just be hindered by familiarity. Great communication goes beyond awareness of the wide variety of tools and traits to encompass the ability to implement it all successfully. It is better characterised by purpose (outcome focus) and adaptability (the ability to help any audience understand any point of view). This is an industry where sophisticated tools and tactics are helpful resources, but longevity and success might be better defined by a little thing called empathy. In the end, this is about 'who' not 'what' we want to be, and the freedom for growth within that mindset is incredible.

Chapter Four highlighted how the young, enthusiastic communicators usually begin their lives fascinated by the complexities and intricacies of meaning – whether they knew it at the time or not. The theories of semantics and semiotics are important, but the reality is that most communicators get the best feel for meaning through practice. In the past, that might have been through different forms of letters and texts, and now it's more illustriously defined by memes, GIFs, emojis and more. Variety here is the undeniable secret to success. By simply acknowledging the way different forms of communication are sent and received in our personal lives, we can more assertively question the validity and necessity of many communications tactics seemingly used 'as standard' in our work. From now on, let's let the meaning dictate the means.

In Chapter Five: Relationship Goals, there was a surprising amount to learn from plucky little plover birds, balance-reading judo experts, and the trials and tribulations of marriage and divorce. As it turns out, it doesn't matter your technical specialism, experience, or lack of either, this work is most valuable when it is relationship-based, and outcome focused. For the former, mutualism is our guide to ensure that both sides benefit from the time and effort spent. And with the latter, the myth-busting realisation that it doesn't matter how charming or funny or kind or helpful or intelligent you are because clients, fundamentally, care about what they are paying you to fix. The

189

difference between success and failure is working with (not for) people to find solutions to their problems. If we all get our heads out of the weeds, and into the minds of the little tooth-picking plover bird, maybe our work would be better than ever.

The 'Jack of All Trades' and my Nana come together in Chapter Six to dispel the bullshit, nonsensical, self-identification that has come to define the modern workforce. Here's an idea, we can all agree on: Chief Ideation Officers et al. are fucking pointless. Instead, we need to bring ourselves back to the core values that built town, industries and nations – that, of course, is "usefulness". The diversity and flexibility required to achieve what a task requires of you, is one of the few prerequisites for success in our ever-changing times. Yet with hyper-specialisation, few have sought to learn a broad enough skills base to be of any use at all. It's not good being a hammer unless every problem you encounter needs a nail. The Swiss, with their multi-tool army knife and incredibly complex mechanical watches, have this really sussed. We all seek to rise up the professional ranks and I do hope all of you who are deserving will. But I also hope that when the time comes, the shots need to be called, and you're the one between your client and a reputation-crushing revelation, you may just find that a 'have and not need, rather than need and not have' approach to learning might just prove a lifesaver.

"You have to be in a state of play to design", said Paula Scher in Chapter Seven, yet we realise that many of us haven't built the basic capabilities to play this game at all. Design, or certainly creative visualisation, has become a critical element to impactful communication in a hyper-distracted world of over-stimulated consumers and audiences. So, while you don't have to spend your days chin-stroking in the art galleries and design studios of your nearest city, you do have to appreciate the role, value and impact of design in the overall success of your communications programs. This is the real outcome-focused approach to communications, where good communicators can rise above to the good, and begin to traipse amongst the great.

Honesty as Policy, I hope, speaks for itself – yet we acknowledge that with a rise of fake news, malicious actors and image-altering technology, it may just be more difficult than ever. We're all suffering from a lack of trust that nobody benefits from, but the good news is that communications professionals have an important role in rebuilding it. How we do that is through integrity in our actions and words, ensuring that honesty and consistency take precedence over the urge for quick-hits and Cannes Lions Awards. For those who fail to heed these warnings, learn from our primate pals, the capuchin monkeys!

The final piece of our complicated (or rather simple, depending on how you look at it) puzzle is, of course, measuring what we do. In Chapter Nine, we expose our deepest, darkest professional flaws, acknowledging that failure to understand our outputs does more disservice than service to our incredibly hard work. We deserve better for ourselves, and of ourselves, and all it will take is a bit of collective thinking. If Eratosthenes could accurately(*ish*) measure the circumference of the earth with a small stick, and Edward Bernays founded the industry on the sole principle of solving business problems, then we can no longer continue to assume that successful communications are marked by the fact that communication has taken place. How exactly we do that, is admittedly up for debate. A debate I'll join with anyone!

****

I'm proud to be part of an industry that is home to hundreds of thousands of bright, hard-working, creative, multi-talented and well-meaning people; with many of us just waiting for the approval to think, act and do better.

The communications industries of the future will be defined by data-driven insights, focused on client-specific needs, and distributed through multi-faceted, audience-defined means. But also, the communications industries of the future will be defined by us, the Tailored Thinkers. If we collectively decide to free ourselves from the self-serving vanity metrics achieved by clickbait, top-tips and "essential" guides, we could actually arrive at the place we all crave – unwavering professional competency, client-servicing credibility, and tangible, valuable impact. Funnily enough, all that's required is to turn our problem-solving obsession to ourselves.

Tailored thinking, then, is an analogical, built-for-purpose, people-obsessed, broadly applicable, outcome-focused approach to solving the communications problems of tomorrow, by taking an unfiltered look at how our practice measures up in the information environment of today. A conversation-starting conversation, if you will, for those of us who have taken on the challenge of joining one of the most diverse, challenging, changeable, frustrating, rewarding, people-focused, technology-obsessed, nation-building, community-dividing, misunderstood industries you could possibly choose to work in.

TAILORED THINKERS started as an insomnia-induced idea, and now stands as the sum of far more thought than writing-time – multiple influences, endless ideation, intense interrogation, rabbit-holes, rewrites, and varied sense-checks. As a result, I gladly say that I haven't written 'the' book on communications, but 'a' book on it.

After all, the type of communications we all benefit from is a conversation. How, then, could I pitch these ideas in any other way?

ENDS

A FINAL NOTE

I always hoped I'd write a book.

But never truly imagined I could have done so at this time in my life, or in this way – without the backing of a traditional publisher, without designers or publicists, without external direction on how it should look or what it should cover.

All I knew is that I wanted to write a book that I would enjoy reading – selfish as that sounds. To do that, it had to be interesting, but not overly detailed; helpful, but doesn't dictate solutions; and short as it possibly can be, without skimping on the value. It's by a busy person, for busy people, and maybe this is going to be a formula for success going forward.

So, whether you agreed or disagreed along the way, make sure to drop me a message on Twitter, Facebook, Instagram or Email. There's much to discuss, and I **think** we can figure it all out, together.

Colm Woods

27435641R00118

Printed in Great Britain
by Amazon